DARK FOLKLORE

MARK NORMAN
AND TRACEY
NORMAN

DARK
FOLKLORE

MARK NORMAN
AND TRACEY
NORMAN

The
History
Press

For our wonderful illustrators,
Tiina and Kathryn,
without whose talent and generosity
this book would look far less beautiful.

Text: Mark Norman and Tracey Norman
Illustrations: Kathryn Avent and Tiina Lilja

First published 2021

The History Press
97 St George's Place, Cheltenham,
Gloucestershire, GL50 3QB
www.thehistorypress.co.uk

British Library Cataloguing in Publication Data.
A catalogue record for this book is available from the British Library.

ISBN 978 0 7509 9801 7

Typesetting and origination by Typo•glyphix
Printed and bound in Great Britain by TJ Books Ltd.

CONTENTS

INTRODUCTION

Most of us love a creepy story. Even if we aren't fans of horror films or literature, there is something about a chilling tale that resonates with us. It can be fun to be a little on edge if it happens in a safe environment.

Look into our history and heritage and there is a rich vein of such stories. Folklore is full of tales of monsters, ghosts and demons. In more superstitious times, before the advent of scientific and medical knowledge that helps us to understand the world, these creatures were seen as responsible for much of what happened to us as a species. The opening chapter of the book demonstrates this clearly.

The internet is full of stories. The digital age has made it easy for people to tell them and pass them on, and they often become embedded in our culture, as you will see in Chapter 4, which examines urban legends. There are many websites talking about those ghosts and hauntings that inspired scary movies or books. Lots of podcasts retell these tales around the virtual campfire.

But what of the historical and social study of these things? Although there are many good books that mention lots of darker tales, there are surprisingly few that offer a more thorough examination of the folklore that informs them. Our reasoning for writing this book was to redress this balance. From ghosts in ancient Greece in Chapter 3 we span the centuries, coming up to date in the twenty-first century with online legends in Chapter 4 and looking at the intersection between our folklore and modern tourism in Chapter 5.

We hope you enjoy this in-depth look into the darker parts of our folkloric past.

ABOUT THE AUTHORS

Tracey Norman is an historian and author. She is the researcher for 'The Folklore Podcast' and writes regular folklore and history columns for *The Moorlander* newspaper. Her stage play, *WITCH* (2016) has been used as Theatre in Education for Years 8 and 9 and Exeter University undergrads and has been included as a formal seminar in two Bristol University undergrad degree courses. Its seventy-fifth performance was also its London premiere. She writes in several genres and is currently working on a supernatural mystery, a non-fiction based on her play, and a fantasy novel.

Mark Norman is a folklore author and researcher, and the creator and host of 'The Folklore Podcast', which can be found online at www.thefolklorepodcast.com. He has previously written *Telling the Bees and Other Customs: The Folklore of Rural Craft* for The History Press as well as other publications on spectral black dogs and fairy lore. Mark is a council member of the Folklore Society and is currently developing a long-term project to bring together a library and archive of folklore materials for future researchers. *The Folklore Library & Archive* can be found at www.folklorelibrary.com.

Tracey and Mark live in Devon, in the south-west of the UK, with their teenage daughter, a trip-hazard cat and some rescue chickens.

ILLUSTRATORS

Tiina Lilja is a Finnish-born visual artist, who is currently living and working in North Devon with her husband and a rescue Alsatian called Shut Up Rusty.

Kathryn Avent is an illustrator from Victoria, Australia. She has a passion for fine-line illustrations with an emphasis on the weird, wonderful and unseen. Drawing inspiration from folklore, fantasy and fairy tales, as well as natural flora and fauna, Kathryn can often be found in the forest looking for stories to draw, flowers to press and treasures to unearth.

Nightmare: Stipple engraving by J.P. Simon, 1810. (Wellcome Collection, CC BY 4.0)

1

THE OLD HAG: FOLKLORE AND SLEEP PARALYSIS

A few years ago, I started having a very strange experience on some nights, waking up during sleep but not feeling awake, could not move and breathed with difficulty. At first, I thought it was a dream, a nightmare in the case, but things started to get worse, became more frequent, even during napping in the school class-room (I was never a very applied student). I went through this situation. It started to scare me. I searched the internet. I visited a doctor; he told me that it was possibly an effect of the combination of stress and deregulated sleep. I worked hard to improve my sleep, started sleeping earlier, regularly, and over time the frequency of 'sleep paralysis' was decreased.[1]

Those words came from one of the listeners to my online folklore programme, 'The Folklore Podcast', in response to a request for information from anyone who had first-hand experience of sleep paralysis.

The medical condition of sleep paralysis is not as unusual as you might think, with statistics suggesting that 8 per cent of the general population have suffered an episode.[2] It occurs as an individual is either entering or leaving the stage of sleep known as REM (or rapid eye movement) and physically presents as an inability to move the limbs, head and torso. In many cases, this may be accompanied by hallucinatory aspects that lead both to fear and a feeling of suffocation or pressure on the chest. Although we understand the medical reasons for the sleep paralysis state now, it has culturally been widely attributed to more superstitious origins, such as visits from demons and other evil spirits in the night, because of these seemingly very real visions.

In the example quoted at the beginning of this chapter, a sufferer describes the physical stage of the condition without touching on any illusory aspects. Even in medical circles, sleep paralysis is often referred to as 'old hag syndrome' because it is common for the hallucinations to take the form of a stereotypical hag as well as the other demonic forms. The imagined creature may appear to sit on your chest and be responsible for the breathing problems. It is this aspect of old hag syndrome that first caused it to enter into folklore and superstition, over the centuries, in similar ways around the world. As we shall see, however, as with most folklore it has developed and adapted over time through association with shifting cultural patterns and the like.

Professor Owen Davies notes that accounts and discussion of sleep paralysis may be found in both European and Chinese writings over the last two millennia, so the experience is far from new.[3] Many sources, including Davies, suggest that the earliest reference to what we now call sleep paralysis may be found around 400 BC in a Chinese book of dreams. This is, however, a little more speculative than it may first appear.

The book in question, *Zhou Li / Chun Guan*, emerged in the pre-Chin period and it noted that the government at that time had set up imperial staff who acted as official dream interpreters. Dreams were placed into six categories, one of which was named '*E-meng*'.

This translates as 'dreams of surprise'. While there is no direct evidence that this category represents sleep paralysis per se, many writers consider that it is similar, with another category, '*Ju-meng*' ('fearful dreams') symbolising nightmares.[4]

A few centuries later, during the Eastern Han dynasty (AD 30–124) the Chinese written character 'yan' appeared in the first Chinese dictionary, *Shuo Wen Chieh Tzu*. This combined the two individual characters for 'ghost' and 'oppression' and is generally taken to mean something along the lines of 'being oppressed by ghost at night and paralysed'.[5]

In less enlightened times it was natural for people to draw on the more supernatural and superstitious beliefs of their culture to explain both the things happening around them and those happening *to* them that they did not understand. This is certainly true of medical conditions before modern treatments and cures began to be discovered and goes some way, for example, to explain the proliferation of folk medicine, charms and spells recorded around the world.

For a person afflicted by sleep paralysis, the experience would naturally be an extremely frightening one. The pressure on the chest may come from breathing difficulties or choking, and so in very early Greek accounts, the phenomenon was known as 'throttling' or 'the throttle'. The earliest recorded case of what is recognisably sleep paralysis is disputed. It has been claimed that the Greek physician, Themison of Laodicea, writing in the first century BC, has the first reference. However, although he refers to the concept of throttling in some letters of the time, there is no clear description of a full case of sleep paralysis.

More likely to have recorded the first true case is seventh-century Byzantine physician Paulus Aeginita. In Section XV of his writings, which examines 'Incubus, or Nightmare' (which we will look at in more detail shortly), he says:

It attacks persons after a surfeit, and who are labouring under protracted indigestion. Persons suffering an attack experience incapacity of motion, a torpid sensation in their sleep, a sense of suffocation, and oppression, as if from one pressing down, with inability to cry out, or they utter inarticulate sounds. Some imagine often that they even hear the person who is going to press them down, that he offers lustful violence to them, but flies when they attempt to grasp him with their fingers.[6]

We certainly find all the common attributes of the state of sleep paralysis in this description, even if medicine has since learned that it is not connected with issues of digestion (although we will pause and look at cheese later!).

Extensive early writings on the phenomenon may also be found in a chapter among the many hundreds that make up the three Persian manuscripts named *Hidayat*, written by the physician Al-Akhawayni Bukhawi. Drawn up in the tenth century, during what was known as the Golden Age of Islamic Medicine, Bukhawi wrote on the subject prior to a description of the condition and treatment of epilepsy.

Often the experience that a person goes through during an episode of sleep paralysis will be accompanied by hypnopompic hallucinations (i.e., those when waking from sleep) or hypnogogic ones (hallucinations experienced when falling asleep), depending on the time at which the sleeper suffers the attack.

The first detailed case study of the condition is probably one published in Latin in a 1664 collection by Dutch physician Isbrand van Diemerbroeck. These works were translated into English in 1689 by William Salmon, a doctor and collector of books. He gave the translation the title *Practical Disputations of Isbrand de Diemerbroeck*. Case History XI was called 'Of the Night-Mare' and reads as follows:

A woman of fifty years of age, in good plight, fleshy, strong and plethoric, sometimes troubled with a headache, and catarrhs falling upon her breast in the winter; the last winter, molested with no catarrhs, but a very sore in the daytime, but in the night time, when she was composing her self to sleep, sometimes she believed the devil lay upon her and held her down, sometimes that she was choaked by a great dog or thief lying upon her breast, so that she could hardly speak or breath, and when she endeavoured to throw off the burthen, she was not able to stir her members. And while she was in that strife, sometimes with great difficulty she awoke of her self, sometimes her husband hearing her make a doleful inarticular voice, waked her himself; at what time she was forced to sit up in bed to fetch her breath; sometimes the same fit returned twice in a night upon her going again to rest.[7]

He continued to make an interesting diagnosis of the condition:

This affection is called Incubus or the Night-Mare, which is an Intercepting of the Motion of the Voice and Respiration, with a false dream of something lying ponderous upon the Breast, the free Influx of the Spirits to the Nerves being obstructed. He thought that due to over-redundancy of blood in the whole body ... the Motion of the Muscles fail ... Now, because the motion of the Muscles, for the most part ceases in time of sleep, except the Respiratory Muscles, therefore the failing of their Motion is first perceived, by reason of the extraordinary trouble that arises for want of Respiration. Now the Patient in her sleep growing sensible of that Streightness, but not understanding the cause in that Condition, believes her self to be overlay'd by some Demon, Thief, or other ponderous Body, being neither able to move her Breast, nor to Breath. The experiences can return the same night: ... that if she fall asleep agin, especially if she lye upon her Back, the same Evil returns ...[8]

The last statement is an interesting one because modern medicine seems to corroborate this idea.

We now have a good understanding of the symptoms. Sleep paralysis is caused when rapid eye movement (REM) sleep is disturbed. Because the body's central nervous system is active at this time, visual and auditory senses are enabled, but because the brain blocks muscle activity during this part of the sleep cycle to prevent injury during dreaming, paralysis is still experienced in the waking state. The sequence of events and resulting hallucinations may come about in the following way.

At the base of the brain lie two almond-shaped clusters of cells called the amygdala. Their name derives from the Latin and translates as 'almond'. Part of the limbic system, this is the area where our emotions are activated and given meaning. Episodes of sleep paralysis could be triggered by an overactive or misfiring amygdala. Something perceived as a 'threat' is triggered subconsciously and so you wake up as part of the natural fight or flight response, but your body is in the wrong sleep cycle and hence you can't move. Your brain cannot accept the paradoxical situation where a threat state has been triggered by the amygdala for no reason, so it generates a hallucinatory one that is probably going to draw either on cultural tropes (witches or demons), an innate fear (maybe spiders or bugs) or an image from something you read recently or a film you watched (such as an alien who may abduct you).

A fourth alternative may be something more random. For example, some people have reported hypnogogic hallucinations of abstract or geometric shapes and one witness recently recorded sleep paralysis events with a hallucination of lines that became tangled – in one case, with numbers appearing on the lines.

To the Chinese (and to many indigenous peoples), spirits are intrinsically linked with the dream state. By way of example, we may consider an obscure case recorded within the Inuit community. The case centres around that of a 30-year-old

Inuit woman who sought help from the Counselling Office of Anchorage Community College. She spoke of how she had suffered from a sleep disorder since she was a young child but had not seen a doctor until she was 18. The woman describes a typical incident in her case notes:

> Just before going to sleep and waking up, I get paralysed. Sometimes it starts with a buzzing. Sometimes I can almost see something and it scares me. My grandparents told me it was a soul trying to take possession of me, and to fight it.
>
> After the buzzing sound I can't move. Sometimes I really start feeling like I am not in my body anymore, like I am outside of my body and fighting to get back. If I don't get back now I never will. I really get panicky. It takes me a long time to move sometimes, like forever. I feel like if I don't get back into my body that I am going to die. That is the first thing that I think of. I finally wake up and move and my heart is just pounding, and I am shaken up and frightened.[9]

Unfortunately, the source for this account does not give any details as to when it took place. We know that it must have happened after 1924 because the doctors, who appeared baffled when told that lots of natives had similar experiences, gave the woman an EEG (electroencephalogram) test before administering Valium and other tranquillisers – the EEG was invented in 1924. It was the doctor who saw the test results who eventually suggested sleep paralysis.

In this case, it appears that the feelings of distress or fear do not come from any hallucination of a spirit or entity, but rather from concern over being trapped in the spirit world. Other native Alaskans who were interviewed about their personal experiences reported similar things.

It is the relationship between the human world and the spirits within Inuit belief that seems to account for the fear in these cases. Native beliefs in Alaska say that one is more susceptible to influence from the spirit realm during sleep, or when entering or leaving that state. While sleeping, the soul is more likely to leave the body because of the chance of outside influence. Paralysis is therefore thought to signify the loss of the soul, with death following if it cannot find its way back and restore movement.

An alternative explanation (for there is generally more than one within folklore) is one of spirit possession, where the paralysis is caused by the entity taking control of the physical body. This is perhaps closer to the Chinese concept of ghost oppression. The Chinese would usually employ the services of a spiritualist when trying to treat the symptoms associated with sleep paralysis. Other cultures took a more medicine-based approach. Greek doctors in early times, for example, would treat the problems with a special diet. We might remember that they believed the condition to be linked to digestive issues. They would also use phlebotomy – what we might more commonly know from the Middle Ages as bloodletting.

In medieval Europe, because of the teachings of the Church, most things that were not seen as good were caused by some form of demonic intervention and so naturally this became the case for the effects of sleep paralysis and its associated hallucinations. Although much more of a patriarchal society in that period, medieval folklore delivers on gender equality from time to time and thus we have the demon in female form preying on sleeping men as well as the reverse – sometimes physically, and sometimes in their dreams.

In the female form, the demon is the succubus, and the name derives from the Old Latin, meaning 'to lie under'. *Sub* (meaning 'under') and *cubare* (the verb 'to lie') become succubare and then succubus, which is also the Medieval Latin term for a prostitute and subsequently applied to the sexual aspects of a demonic visit in the night.

In modern times we tend to use the word nightmare to refer to any particularly bad dream. It may wake us with a start, or in a cold sweat, but by the morning it may be mostly forgotten. The roots of the term nightmare, however, refer to something rather worse. Proto-Indo-European etymology gives us '*mor*' (a malicious female spirit) and '*mer*', the verb 'to die'. This developed all over Europe into '*mare*' (for example, in Old and Middle English and Scottish) and '*mara*' (from the Old Norse, across Iceland, Scandinavia and into Germanic and Old Saxon language). In Croatia, the term for sleep paralysis is '*Mora*', which again comes from similar linguistic roots.

Mara may also be seen to derive from the verb '*merran*', meaning 'crusher'. Certainly, this linguistic root taken alongside those above describes the attributes of a creature sitting on the chest of one sleeping at night and causing them to be paralysed. While not strictly demonic in the ways later described by the Christianised Church version, the Norse *mara* is therefore a magical creature that rides its victim for nefarious pleasure.

Grendel, one of three monsters in the epic Anglo-Saxon poem *Beowulf*, is referred to twice using the term '*maere*'. This makes good sense in the context of the creature's preferred method of attacking men while they sleep, who it crushes and tears apart. Before Beowulf faces Grendel, it is explained that others have been beaten because they were unable to stay awake during the night:

> what sudden harryings. Hall-folk fail me,
> my warriors wane; for Wyrd hath swept them
> into Grendel's grasp. But God is able
> this deadly foe from his deeds to turn!
> Boasted full oft, as my beer they drank,
> earls o'er the ale-cup, armed men,
> that they would bide in the beer-hall here,
> Grendel's attack with terror of blades.
> Then was this mead-house at morning tide
> dyed with gore, when the daylight broke,
> all the boards of the benches blood-besprinkled,

gory the hall: I had heroes the less,
doughty dear-ones that death had reft.[10]

Grendel is described elsewhere in the poem as being a descendant of Cain, an important point to which we will return in a moment.

The Latin term for the nightmare is '*incubo*' and it is from this root that we see the development of the incubus in medieval superstition. The incubus was said to be a male demon who would lie with sleeping women and have intercourse with them. They were able to father children, an aspect that was undoubtedly used to explain illegitimate or unwanted pregnancies. The half-demon child of a woman and an incubus was known as a 'cambion'. Merlin, the sorcerer of King Arthur's legendary court, was said to have been the result of an incubus sleeping with his mother. This was the way in which he obtained his magical skills.

In both cases, the incubus and succubus were used to explain the symptoms of sleep paralysis and night terrors because the demon would sit on the victim's chest, pinning them down so they couldn't move and hampering their breathing. There are some suggestions also that these creatures were associated with less savoury experiences such as sexual dreams, night-time sexual attacks or advances by trusted people such as relatives or members of the Church.

Records suggest that women were attacked by incubi far more than men were by succubi and hence legends say that there was only one succubus to every nine incubi. Of course, this may be because the method of impregnation requires the incubus to work harder in the manner of a worker bee. The *Malleus Maleficarum* tells how the succubus would collect semen from the male victim, which the incubus would then take around to impregnate human women. This was how demons, traditionally impotent, were said to be able to reproduce and father children as noted above.

King James, who wrote extensively on witches, demons and more in his tract *Daemonologie*, had slightly differing views. He agreed

DÆMONOLOGIE,
IN FORME
OF A DIA-
LOGVE,

Diuided into three books:

WRITTEN BY THE HIGH
and mightie Prince, I A M E S by the
grace of God King of England,
Scotland, France *and* Ireland,
Defender of the Faith, &c.

LONDON,
Printed by *Arnold Hatfield* for
Robert VVald-graue.
1 6 0 3

Title page of Daemonologie, *by King James I. (Wellcome Collection, CC BY 4.0)*

that angels and demons as entities were incapable of reproduction, but then his suggestion was that the devil would intervene and use one of two methods to put seed into the human female. This would either be demonic intervention or possession.

In the former case, King James postulated that the incubus and succubus were actually the same entity – two sides of the same demonic coin – transporting semen and impregnating the victim and essentially appearing differently in each stage of the process. In the latter case, the devil would actually enter a dead male body and cause it to rise by possession. In this state, the corpse may be found to be able to engage in intercourse with the living female. What James does not seem to suggest, however, is that this worked in reverse as an explanation for cases where a female entity engaged in unwanted relations with a male victim.

We may find parallels to the succubus as a demon who offers temptation to men in other cultures. In Islamic traditions this creature is called the 'Qarinah' and in old Middle Eastern superstitions it is known as 'Lilith', a name that is used for a seductress in some versions of the Bible. The Qarinah, according to Arabian mythology, is generally said to be invisible to anyone who does not have the gift of second sight. In those cases where it can be seen, the Qarinah will appear in animal form, usually as a cat or dog, or some other domestic pet. This would suggest links to the Islamic supernatural beings often called the *jinn*, who are described as appearing in three forms, one of which is zoomorphic.

In Biblical terms Lilith was, according to Jewish mythology, Adam's first wife. Prior to Eve, who the Book of Genesis tells us was fashioned by God from one of Adam's ribs, Lilith was created at the same time, and from the same clay, as him. Lilith and Adam, however, argued because Lilith refused to be subservient and to lie under Adam, insisting that they should be equal. She said (in what can be seen as a direct parallel with the succubus lore) that she would rather lie on top. After Adam said that this could not be the case, Lilith left the Garden of Eden. Adam told God that his wife had left, leading to God fashioning the replacement Eve with help from Adam.

Later, on returning to the Garden, Lilith discovers that she has been replaced by Eve. Mystical literature written by early Jews says that she torments Adam in his sleep, but prior to this she attacks the couple's firstborn son, Cain (in the manner of a succubus in its medieval Latin translation). As a result of this, she bears a number of demons and spirits.[11] You will recall that the cannibalistic Grendel was described in *Beowulf* as being a descendant of Cain.

We can see that many cultures and traditions use the image of the 'mare' or demon in order to bring understanding to a condition about which nothing would have been known medically. And this is one of the aspects of folklore generally that should be of great interest to us. Why do we find similar motifs employed in so many different countries and cultures and how do they travel?

One answer to this question may follow the ideas of Jungian psychology. The concept suggests that we all carry some form of collective subconscious upon which we may draw when we decode symbols around us. It may have been developed throughout the evolution of our species and can be considered to be a kind of folk memory. Our brain may make use of this independently of our commonplace normal thinking or at times when we are not engaged in wakeful thought.

Another theory that has been proposed to explain why we see similarities in different supernatural experiences is known as the 'cultural source hypothesis'. This idea suggests that the stories and traditions in a particular culture may shape the ideas that people from that culture have about the world in general and hence their experiences within it. Where this hypothesis is somewhat limiting is in the fact that it only works for one distinct culture at a time.

In his book on sleep paralysis, *The Terror that Comes in the Night*, University of Pennsylvania Professor David Hufford proposes an alternative theory that he calls the 'experiential source hypothesis'. Here, Hufford suggests that some elements of supernatural events are, in fact, universal and not related to culture at all. Similarly, anthropologist Michael Winkelman believes that humans are hard-wired to see spirits genetically. He calls this concept 'neurotheology' and discusses it with particular reference to shamans but extends the idea to us generally as a species.[12] The idea of neurotheology doesn't take as its premise the idea that spirits are real, but rather that the experiences that people have with them are authentic.

One country that does have a long tradition of ghost belief and a complex structure of ghost-types, which they call the Yōkai, is Japan. 'Yōkai' is a general term for the wide variety of ghosts and other supernatural beings that we find in this country. They appear in many old myths and legends but also, because of their proliferation, we find that in different stories they are quite often contradictory in their nature. Such is the way with folklore!

The Japanese have their own term for sleep paralysis: *Kanashibari*. The English translation of this is 'bound in metal', referring obviously to the inability to move the body during a paralysis episode. Stories of *Kanashibari* can be traced back to ancient times and are equated with a supernatural force entering the body itself. Different legends highlight differing causes, but the most common type is one of possession. In these cases, the body is invaded by any one of several forms of *tsukimono*, the Japanese term for animal spirits.

In some of the Japanese folk tales, *Kanashibari* can be caused not by animals or ghosts, but by magicians or priests. Even in modern times, there can sometimes be a religious connection to the experience. For example, in one case recorded in 1987, a witness said, 'I suddenly woke up from sleep and found that I couldn't move a bit. I couldn't speak either. I saw a figure, which resembled a Buddhist image, on my stomach. I was very frightened.'[13]

Another Yōkai that is equated with *Kanashibari* is the Makura-gaeshi. The translation of this is 'pillow-flipper', referring to the spirit's habit of moving the pillows from the head to the foot of the bed overnight. As you might gather from this, the Makura-gaeshi is seen as a form of trickster spirit. Dressed as a monk, or a samurai, it might do things such as running through ash from the fire and leaving dirty footprints all over the house.

Makura-gaeshi. (Illustration by Kathryn Avent)

The Makura-gaeshi haunts rooms at night and is connected in *Kanashibari* with the symptom of pressure on the chest that we equate with Western definitions of sleep paralysis. In this form of *Kanashibari*, it is the ghost of a small child that is seen sitting on the chest of the sufferer.

Where *Kanashibari* differs from Western sleep paralysis interpretations is in the notion that it is not seen as a dream. This is because Japanese culture has a slightly different conceptual framework to it. Because *Kanashibari* is representative of a supernatural force, Japanese spiritualists warn that people should be careful if they experience it, because it demonstrates that there are spirits nearby, or that they are trying to communicate with the person in the mortal realm. In other words, we might see *Kanashibari* as a 'sixth sense', warning us of supernatural creatures.

The liminal time between sleep and wakefulness is of great interest to us as folklorists, as are other boundary states – a time when things are neither one form nor the other. The times when we are entering or leaving the dream state, the hypnogogic and hypnopompic periods, are times that are ripe for potential hallucinatory experiences. They are the points at which we may see or experience odd sensations and hence are common times for reports of ghostly encounters or alien abductions. This is precisely the reason why it is of such interest when symbols or motifs referenced over time are so similar. Are we drawing on shared subconscious imagery? Is this the reason that an image such as the mare is recurring?

The most common recurring image referenced after the medieval period with regards to the hallucinations associated with sleep paralysis is that of the old hag. This draws upon the stereotypical image of the witch. So, how did the folklore move on from the demonic creatures of the medieval period to that of the hag?

Of equal interest to us is where this imagery links in with, draws from or informs other folkloric motifs. In some areas of folklore this is quite common. In the case of old hag syndrome, it is more unusual, but we do find it.

In personal correspondence, Andrew D. Gable wrote of his experiences with sleep paralysis. He said:

> Though I've had sleep disturbances quite a few times, I've only had 'true' sleep paralysis once. I awoke around 2:30 or 3 in the morning with a feeling of dread and fear; I didn't have the 'typical' Old Hag encounter with the strangling entity sitting on the chest, but I did see a shadowy human figure (much like the 'shadow people' of modern lore) standing in the corner of my room about 10 feet from my bed. Its hands were held rigidly at its sides like a soldier standing at attention. After a short time, I managed to blink a few times and the figure gradually faded from view.

In this case, we have the common aspects of fear upon waking but the demonic entity on the chest is replaced with more ghostly apparitional symbols. Other researchers suggest that the old hag experience may be responsible for a number of UFO abduction experiences (and by extension, possibly some fairy experiences). At the end of this chapter, we will return to this point and look at how some other people's experiences draw on more modern cultural symbols to decode the experience of their sleep paralysis.

We may sometimes find regional variations in the folklore of other countries when we come to look at the old hag. In Newfoundland, for example, an area rich in folklore and tradition, the belief is that your enemy may be responsible for sending the hag to attack you while you sleep.

In other countries the folklore of the old hag phenomenon is mixed with many other symbols or tropes. In Hungarian folklore, for instance, we find the Liderc. This creature may take one of several forms, but in each case, it is said to hatch from the first egg of a black hen; the egg having been kept warm either in a pile of manure or in a human's armpit. The creature that emerges from the egg might be a form of imp, it might be a variant of a form of magic chicken or in some cases a fully grown person. In this latter case, it may even be a person who was known to the owner of the Liderc, such as a deceased member of their family or a past lover.

In many ways the Liderc behaves in the same way as the incubus or succubus but the person who owns one is also considered to be making some kind of pact with the devil. Where the Liderc as an example of sleep paralysis becomes really interesting is that the motif demonstrates crossover with other areas of folklore. For example, the Liderc periodically climbs onto the chest of its owner

Liderc. (Illustration by Kathryn Avent)

in the manner of normal old hag experiences, but then it is said to drink their blood, weakening them, as in vampire lore.

As an aside, we may find paralysis mentioned in one of the most famous of all vampire stories, Bram Stoker's *Dracula*, where the arrival of the count is described:

> There was in the room the same thin white mist that I had before discovered ... I felt the same vague terror which had come to me before and the same sense of some presence ... Then indeed, my heart sank within me. Beside the bed, as if it had stepped out of the mist ... or rather as if the mist had turned into his figure, for it had completely disappeared ... stood a tall, thin man all in black. I knew him at once from the description of the others. The waxen face, the high aquiline nose, on which the light fell in a thin white line; the parted red lips, with the sharp white teeth showing between, and the red eyes ... I would have screamed out, only that I was paralysed.

In this case, of course, the paralysis may be seen to be caused as much by fear as by the more regular symptoms of sleep paralysis.

Another folkloric crossover can be found in the method of destroying the Liderc. The only way to successfully do this is to instruct it to perform an impossible task. We find similarities here with the binding of the deceased to impossible tasks in death for retribution against their deeds in life – this being common in Western folklore. The Liderc will literally implode from frustration while trying to perform its task.

Along similar lines to the etymology of the mare discussed earlier, in Hungarian, the term for nightmare is *Lidercnyomas*. This translates as 'Liderc pressure', relating to the paralysis aspect.

Sleep paralysis as a phenomenon is not unusual. As we have seen, around 8 per cent of the world's population will experience it at least once. As well as being common in sleep disorders such as narcolepsy it can also be brought on by sleep deprivation. The body paralysis that prevents us acting out dreams in REM sleep continues into partial wakefulness in an episode, which can last up to six minutes.

It is not always the case that people have the hallucinatory aspect of sleep paralysis, but where they do, the creature that they see will be drawn from the cultural upbringing of the individual. The dream state is one that links our deep memories and metaphors from the world around us. In this way, it tends to support the archetypal psychology of researchers such as Carl Jung. It is clear that the tension between the ideas of cultural source and experiential source hypothesis is very real. I would suggest that, in the case of folklore connected to sleep paralysis at least, the best-fit psychological approach to employ lies somewhere in the middle of the two. Culture, and certainly mass media, definitely inform the experience.

Other cultures that refer to the creature on the chest motif include Germanic lore, where it is referred to as an Alp and an attack by the creature as an *Alpdruck*, and Appalachian cultures where, if you wake on your back and cannot breathe, it is said that 'the hag is riding your chest'.

Sleeping on your back has been medically linked with the onset of a sleep paralysis episode. As well as superstitious traditions such as placing a broom by the door and putting a pile of sand on the bed (to compel the intruder to count the grains in the same manner as vampire lore), Italian cures for sleep paralysis also included sleeping face down.

Waking on your back, a link found in Appalachian beliefs, was the trigger for the first experience of another personal correspondent, who asked to be referred to as just Steve. Steve is 46 and lives outside Nashville, Tennessee.

On the first occasion, where Steve was lying on his back, he says that he was trying to scream but could not make any sound. He forced himself to calm down and stopped trying to actively do anything for a short while. Then he took a deliberate breath and tried to scream again, but once again there were no results. As suddenly as it had all begun, it seemed to be over. Whoever or whatever Steve felt had been with him was gone. He was able to move and to sit up in bed and collect himself, although he was quite shaken from the experience.

On another occasion (Steve thinks perhaps the second or third time it happened), he awoke to find himself lying on his left side with his back close to the edge of the bed. He reports that he felt a female presence standing behind him at the bedside. This felt more like a kindly feminine entity rather than an old hag and Steve thinks that she was trying to straighten the bedsheets over him. Although Steve acknowledges that this is somewhat different to the traditional old hag accounts, he was still unable to move at the time and it was only when he felt the sensation that the presence was gone that he was able to move.

It is interesting that the presence in the room seemed to be nurturing rather than demonic or frightening, while the paralysis symptom remained the same. Possibly Steve is fortunate in that his brain deals with the out-of-place REM-induced paralysis in a different and more positive way. Steve does say in his notes, however, that the experience was still unsettling because, although it felt like somebody was with him, there was no physical being in the room.

Seeing multiple figures or creatures is unusual in terms of old hag syndrome and historic folklore examples tend to cite a single creature. Although the paralysis angle is present, the figures act differently. Steve's experience with a more benevolent aspect is also very rare, as most sleep paralysis cases that refer to hallucinations, or the appearance of non-physical forms, tend to be frightening.

It is not, however, unique. Another sufferer of sleep paralysis episodes, Joana Varanda, again writing in personal correspondence, also described some positive experiences:

> In the same moments between sleeping and waking, I have sometimes felt the opposite way: with an overwhelming feeling of happiness, hope. Inflated with a sudden and sure 'everything will be alright' pure knowledge. The first time it happened, I was in my early teens. My hand was hanging from my bed and a little girl appeared and held it. Here's where it gets weird: she told me her name, and that she would soon be born. A short while later, I found that a distant relative was pregnant with a girl. But to this day, I still haven't met her.
>
> The second time, I was 27, it was the same feeling of pure joy and hope, but this time it was a little boy. The room was illuminated as if suddenly dozens of candles had been lit. I felt warm and loved, and when I woke up later in the morning, the light on the bedside table was turned on, but I was sure I'd turned it off before going to bed.
>
> The third time was quite recently actually, when I moved to my new house, it felt like the same boy from before was holding my hand and telling me all would be well. The room felt lit up again.

When we reach the early modern period of our history, a time rich in folkloric stories connected with witchcraft, we see a firm link form between aspects of sleep paralysis and alleged bewitchment. Of all the things that led to accusations of witchcraft at this time – sickness in animals, ill fortune and so on – the most likely causes would be where the victim suffered physical trauma or mental illness. Often coupled with these would be the supernatural visionary appearance of the witch to the victim, usually in the bed chamber at night. We find it reported in Salem, in the witch trials of Scotland and in many other examples. Where a physical attack is said to follow, we find a direct parallel with later old hag appearances in paralysis episodes. The hag trope leads neatly from these earlier accusations.

We have previously discussed the etymology of the mare, much of which refers to the pressure on the chest of the sleeper. Over time, in some cultures the language took on the witch aspect more explicitly. The German *hexendrucken*, for example, translates as 'witch-pressing' and the Hungarian *boszorkany-nyomas* also means 'witches' pressure'. The similar idea of being straddled, emerging from the earlier sexual demon lore, leads to the terms 'witch-ridden' or 'hag-ridden' in both England and Newfoundland, where folklore of the old hag is particularly strong.

Because the rise of herbalists, wise women and other traditional practitioners in the early modern period began to lead to a mistrust of the figure of the witch, it was inevitable that this figure should come to represent supernatural evil, so the incubus and succubus naturally came to be replaced as the cause or scapegoat in paralysis episodes. The folklore associated with the mare and the witch began to combine and morph into characters such as the *morica*, from Dalmatian beliefs; a girl who was born with a red caul and became a witch when she married, or the Polish *zmora* – a living person who would visit others in their sleep in the same manner as the old hag. Even the Norwegian *mara* shows witchcraft parallels where she may be one of seven daughters. We find the motif of the 'seventh' frequently in witch lore, and folklore more generally, as a magical number.

As the folklore changes and reshapes, in the fluid way that beliefs do, the image of a witch as an old hag in this phenomenon begins to be cited more often in witch trial transcripts. Most people will have at least some familiarity with the happenings in Salem, Massachusetts, in this respect. One of the women accused was Susanna Martin. Bernard Peach's deposition tells how she 'came in and jumped down upon the floor. She took hold of this deponent's feet, and drawing his body up into an heap, she lay upon him near two hours; in all which time he could neither speak nor stir.'

Many of the English and Scottish trials follow similar lines. Even where the physical aspects are not listed so explicitly, the language suggests that depositions are referring to old hag syndrome. Testimony against Ann Wagg in 1650 says that it was known that a sick child was witch-ridden because she could not speak. There are multiple examples where victims dispel an attack by making the sign of the cross with their tongue because the rest of their body is paralysed.

Although old hag syndrome provided confirmation of bewitching for victims in less-enlightened times, the courts and lawyers were relatively cautious about accepting the evidence. Of course, nothing can stand in the way of moral panic, as the Salem trials aptly demonstrated.

Interestingly, in parallel, some began to see the phenomenon as a medical condition around the same time. Elizabethan sceptic Reginald Scot said, 'in truth, this Incubus is a bodily disease'. Swiss Minister Ludwig Laveter, writing on nocturnal spirits, made a similar observation.

One 'medical' (with the term firmly in inverted commas) explanation for nightmares, traditionally, is that cheese causes them due to its indigestible nature. It is therefore very much linked to this phenomenon. The motif of the witch 'riding' a victim may be traced right back to the writings of Homer and can be seen as having an ambiguous meaning. Cheese in folklore often signifies both women and sex. Apuleius uses the term to denote women as sexual partners in the same way that 'crumpet' is used as British slang. Shakespeare uses it in *The Merry Wives of Windsor* and the Grimm brothers note that German monks were known as cheese-hunters in medieval times. In Britain, two women kissing were known as 'cheese and cheese'.

In the year 1204 an Irish chieftain, who became known as Cheese-Guzzler O'Ruairc, died of a 'surfeit of sex'. Although his partner was most definitely flesh and blood, the manner of the event shows marked similarities to the symbol of the witch mare. This cheese symbolism relates back to the same interpretations of the mare as incubi attacks. Hildegard of Bingen attributed these sexual aspects to the demon exploiting the trace of sin left behind from the act of intercourse that caused that person's conception. She also referred to this as coagulation, which again harks to cheese making.

You may recall that early Greek attempts at diagnosis of the symptoms of sleep paralysis suggested that it was connected to the digestive system. More links between indigestion, often caused by cheese, and the old hag attack come from Scandinavian tradition, where we also find more interesting etymological ties. Here, the creature known as the 'hug' denoted desire or will and was an aspect of the self that could affect others' bodies. From the hug we find the term *hig* in northern English dialect, meaning a fit of passion. A powerful hug could cause cattle to sicken or milk to sour in the manner of accusations of bewitching. The strongest was a *rehug*, which translates as 'riding hug', and visits people in a nightmare. The hug could appear in various forms including a thick mist. Interestingly, in northern England, a thick mist is called a hag.

We find sexual aspects of night visitations in some of the witch trial documents and these naturally draw on the older demonic lore of the incubus and succubus. The sexual element is actually much older than this, as the quote from Paulus Aeginita showed.

Earlier in the chapter, I suggested that incubus lore was drawn on as a way of explaining attacks by figures in authority. This is the case in a 1640 episode of sexual attack and alleged possession from Louviers, where a priest, Father Picard, molested some of the nuns. After the attacks, one reported how 'a tremendous weight rested on my shoulders so that I thought I was going to choke'. Another said she found the incubus of a cat in indecent postures, with a huge penis like a man's.

Demonic sexual attack was reported to be an unpleasant affair. It was uncomfortable and the devil's semen was said to be extremely cold. This is borne out not only in medieval witch trial transcripts but also in modern sleep paralysis surveys.

Records of men describing sexual activity in paralysis episodes are rarer, but Professor Owen Davies highlights a good one from the year 1684.[14] A footman employed by a West Country noble was observed lying in bed, with staring eyes and in a violent sweat after having been sent to bed with a headache. When he woke, he described two women who had entered his chamber:

> They endeavoured to come into the bed with him. He resisted with all the power he could, striking at them several times with his fists, but could feel nothing but empty shadows. He had contested so long with them that he concluded within himself he should die under their violences, during all that time he had no power to speak, or call for aid.

The roots of the incubus and succubus motif may come at least in part from the ancient Greek. Here the Empusae were the demonic daughters of the goddess Hecate. They were said to be able to turn themselves into bitches, cows or beautiful maidens (reminiscent of the maiden, mother, crone aspects of the triple goddess with which Hecate may be associated). In these forms they would lie with men at night and suck the life from them. There are similarities here with the Hungarian Liderc.

There is no doubt that sleep paralysis, or old hag syndrome, is a very real condition that can be, and often is, terrifying for the sufferer. The fact that we now understand the causes of it does not make the actual experience any easier to bear. The modern fear is less associated with the inability to move, for which the medical reasons are well known, but more for the fact that the brain naturally draws on imagery that scares us when rationalising this paralysis. This means that as well as the traditional witches and demons, more modern images cause the folklore to evolve over time.

Psychologist Dr Susan Blackmore, who specialises in anomalous experiences, highlights in work undertaken in 2000 that alien abduction is often part of the modern sleep paralysis myth.[15] Blackmore, and her co-author Marcus Cox, note:

> Most experiences begin in bed at night ... The abductee experiences an intense blue or white light, a buzzing or humming sound, anxiety and the sense of an unexplained presence. He or she is then transported or 'floated' into a craft and may be restrained or paralysed and subjected to examinations, medical procedures, or the implantation of a small object in the nose or elsewhere. The aliens are typically grey, about four feet high, with a large head and black almond shaped eyes, though other aliens are occasionally reported.

The image of the alien (especially the one in this description) is one that we can trace back a long way. It emerges from much older fairy lore, morphing with the influence of science fiction in the media. There are many parallels between being taken by the fairies and being abducted by aliens. In the internet age, we find that these characters are beginning to morph once again, driven especially by the popularity of the Creepypasta, taken from the website of the same name and explored in detail in Chapter 4.

Creepypastas are legends with a horror theme that have circulated, been added to and increased in popularity through their copying and pasting across the internet. The name Creepypasta itself derives from the term 'copypasta' – internet terminology for copied and pasted text. The image of Slenderman is a prime example of this. In the case of that character, we know the originator of the legend by name, but this is not always the case and sometimes the lines are very blurred between what might be considered to be an invented supernatural creature and one that is considered more superstitiously 'real'.

There is some evidence to suggest that the figure of the alien, with relation to sleep paralysis, is also developing to include experiences with 'Shadow People'. Shadow People are said to be supernatural entities who appear in the periphery of one's vision, fading away or passing through a wall when noticed. We might consider the character of 'The Silence' from the rebooted *Doctor Who* television series to be heavily influenced by the Shadow People, as well as by Slenderman, with their mode of dress. Many modern sleep paralysis episodes have been described that include images of these creatures.

Jung, in discussing the idea of the shadow, referred to it as the dark part of ourselves and the part being kept hidden by our conscious minds. Psychologist Michelle Goddard notes that the Shadow People are the embodiment of the defences that we all have because our shadow also acts as a defence mechanism. Both statements seem to resonate with why they might occur in a sleep paralysis hallucination.

Some people believe that the Shadow People are inter-dimensional, extra-terrestrial beings – that is, they come from another universe, and this may certainly feed into the development of the imagery from fairies, to aliens and now in this direction.

Another correspondent who suffered with hallucinations that seemed to draw on both Creepypastas and other horror media is Victoria Pohlen, who described to me in an email a sleep paralysis episode that drew on a creature that was a cross between Slenderman and the Babadook (the titular monster from a 2014 Australian psychological horror film). Victoria wrote:

> I actually have never seen the movie *The Babadook*, but a friend told me extensively about the plot, and around the third and most recent instance where the form of the terror was much clearer, the image in the storybook of the Babadook from the movie was circulating a lot on

tumblr, which I used daily at that point in time, so I was used to seeing it several times a week, mostly as a joke. The third instance I remember the most clearly because I wasn't at home, I was traveling, and my mother and I were staying with some family friends. We and our host had watched an episode of some crime show or other (not NCIS or SVU, if you're from the US/familiar with American television, but think along those lines), and the end of the episode involved a shot of some missing persons' corpses below the sand in a desert where they'd been buried by their murderer. My mom and I were staying in a guest room with two beds and we went to bed basically right after watching that episode. I woke up a few hours later, and was immediately aware of the sensation of the thing looming over me - tall and pale, and lots of tentacley arms, but with a hat and a face like the Babadook, and more claws on the tentacles than Slenderman is known for.

I was laying on my side facing the bed my mother was in, and I was so convinced that if I moved at all, I would be gobbled up. I could feel the presence behind me almost as a physical force, as if it was looming inches from my back. I felt like if I focused harder on it and not literally anything else, I'd be able to feel breath on my neck. My eyes wouldn't even blink, and my mouth got dried out because I was breathing through my mouth and couldn't swallow or close it. I felt like maybe I'd swoon from being sweaty before I had to wait for the feeling to pass. I was 21 at the time, so by the time the feeling did start to pass (I don't know what stops it, maybe the adrenaline running out after a while? but it starts to fade, though I couldn't begin to tell you the timeframe on that), I had also gotten over my embarrassment of trying to wake my mom up as a full adult to tell her I was having a nightmare, so I managed finally to whisper loudly enough to wake her up, and she was not pleased. She told me it wasn't real and to go back to bed, and then I was re-embarrassed enough that the spell was well and truly broken, and I was able to finally take a terrified peek over my shoulder to discover that nothing was there, and eventually I calmed down enough to fall back asleep.

Victoria had suffered two previous experiences before this one. The first featured a 'generic teeth and claws' image, followed by a second relating to Slenderman. During the first, Victoria described the fact that she was sweating, and her muscles were cramping because her brain was telling her that she couldn't move. Victoria suffers from Tourette's Syndrome and yet this experience overpowered the constant movements her body normally makes because of that affliction. Of course, the brain is a complex organ that we do not, and may never, fully understand and sometimes it might draw on some rather more 'left-field' examples from our culture during a sleep paralysis episode.

Deborah Hyde, former editor of the critical-thinking publication *The Skeptic Magazine*, has suffered from many sleep paralysis episodes. As well as the traditional hallucinations of witch-like characters, Deborah also recalled one hallucination where the creature that appeared was a metal 'Smash alien'.

Smash is a brand of instant mashed potato in the United Kingdom, launched in the 1960s by Cadbury, a company who are more usually associated with confectionery. During the 1970s and 1980s, the product was advertised on television using a family of alien robot characters who monitored the Earth and mocked the human inhabitants who laboriously prepared and boiled potatoes rather than using the Smash instant mashed potato product that the aliens had. The characters became iconic at the time and were later voted 'TV advert of the century' by *Campaign* magazine.

Deborah can offer no explanation as to why this particular character appeared in her hallucination, but she does note that it 'had a real sense of menace' that she didn't get with the more traditional motifs. This may be because, as a researcher into witchcraft, Deborah is so used to the themes that there is no sense of 'other', whereas the unexpected appearance of a robotic potato alien definitely puts one on edge.

Another witness reported that their hallucination was of Shaggy, from the 'Mystery Incorporated' *Scooby Doo* gang, standing panicking in the corner of their bedroom. Maybe Velma would have been able to provide an explanation for this one if she had been there too!

REFERENCES

1   Personal correspondence, Anonymous.
2   Olunu, E. et al., 'Sleep Paralysis, a Medical Condition with a Diverse Cultural Interpretation'. *International Journal of Applied Basic Medical Research*, July–September 2018.
3   Davies, O., 'The Nightmare Experience, Sleep Paralysis, and Witchcraft Accusations', *Folklore*, Vol. 114, No. 2, August 2003.
4   Wing, Y. et al., 'Sleep Paralysis in Chinese Ghost Oppression Phenomenon in Hong Kong', *Sleep*, 17(7) (1994).
5   Chang, C.Y. and W. Lin (eds), *The Encyclopaedic Dictionary of the Chinese Language* (Taipei: College of Chinese Cultural Press, 1966).
6   Paulus (Aegineta), Adams, F. (trans.), *The Seven Books of Paulus Aegineta: Translated from the Greek, with a Commentary Embracing a Complete View of the Knowledge Possessed by the Greeks, Romans and Arabians on All Subjects Connected with Medicine and Surgery*, Vol. 1 (1844).
7   Van Diemerbroeck, I., *The Anatomy of Human Bodies. Comprehending the Most Modern Discoveries and Curiosities in that Art. To Which is added a Particular Treatise of the Small Pox and Measles. Together with several Practical Observations and Experienc'd Cures* (London: 1689).
8   *Ibid.*
9   Bloom, J. and R. Gelardin, 'Eskimo Sleep Paralysis', *Arctic*, Vol. 29, 1 March 1976.
10 Anonymous, Grummere, F.B. (trans.), *Beowulf*, via www.poetryfoundation.org (accessed 10 October 2019).
11 Adler, S.R., 'Sleep Paralysis: Night-Mares, Nocebos, and the Mind-Body Connection', *Studies in Medical Anthropology* (Rutgers University Press, 2011).
12 Winkelman, M., *Shamanism: A Biopsychosocial Paradigm of Consciousness and Healing* (Praeger, 2010).
13 Fukuda, K., et al., 'High Prevalence of Isolated Sleep Paralysis: *Kanashibari* Phenomenon in Japan', *Sleep*, Vol. 10, Issue 3 (1987).
14 Davies, O. 'The Nightmare Experience, Sleep Paralysis, and Witchcraft Accusations', *Folklore*, Vol. 114, No. 2, August 2003.
15 Blackmore, S. and M. Cox, 'Alien Abductions, Sleep Paralysis and the Temporal Lobe', *European Journal of UFO and Abduction Studies* (2000).

Dark Church. (Illustration by Tiina Lilja)

2

BLURRING THE LINES: THE DARK CHURCH

When we think of a church, we will think of it in a variety of ways, depending on who we are and on our beliefs. A place of worship, a sacred space to remember those who have passed, somewhere for quiet reflection. Sanctity.

For some, though, the church holds a different appeal. A place of otherworldly mystery, haunted by the spirits of those who have passed, the church is viewed as a liminal space where the veil between our world and the next is thin and can often be breached. A power source.

Those who frequented churches left their mark, either physically, as we see in the graffiti scored into the fabric of the buildings themselves, or in anecdotes, spells and rituals. These may not have left any physical sign – something that is important to magical practitioners – but are instead preserved in grimoires, spell books and explorations of the history of magic and witchcraft.

Looking around a church today, we are likely to find any amount of what could be classed as 'non-Christian' imagery, from mermaids to Green Men to ships to heraldic symbolism. Some have been incised into the stones or woodwork of the church by its attendees, but others adorn pew ends and ceiling bosses, indicating that they have particular significance within the church. As ever, when trying to decode the intent of those who have gone before us, the path is murky and the records scant. In the end, all we can do is make a best guess in most cases, based on what little evidence we have. These interpretations will undoubtedly evolve over time as we continue to explore and analyse.

Churches are thresholds between the living and the dead, between man and God, between magic and the mundane and, it could be argued, between the rich and poor. We have only to look at the memorials and imagery in the stained-glass windows to see that it is the church's wealthy patrons who are commemorated, those able to afford the cost of a headstone or a marble plaque detailing their connections and achievements. The poor and the ordinary citizen, although far outnumbering the wealthy, are almost entirely absent, their lives passing without leaving any permanent mark on their world except their line of descendants.

Yet if we examine our churches more closely, we will start to see evidence that this is not entirely true. Scratched into the stone are snapshots of the past, records of the beliefs of members of the congregation. Unlike today, where graffiti is seen as vandalism and frowned upon, in times past, this was not the case. There are numerous examples of images carved at different times and carefully positioned so as not to overlap existing graffiti, indicating consideration for what was already present. The fact that we can see these images at all indicates that they were not painted over or otherwise removed, and thus that they had a recognised and acceptable significance within the early modern Church. Champion (2015) describes them as '... clearly devotional or votive in nature and a far cry from the random doodling of an alienated generation. They were the prayers, memorials, hopes and fears of the medieval parish.'[1]

The secular nature of church graffiti partly explains the numerous non-religious images. Those creating the carvings were using imagery with special significance to them, and thus are likely to have been influenced by superstition and their daily lives as much as by the Church. Many of these people left no records behind, and of those who did, there would be no mention of why a mermaid, for example, held significance for them. In a society where illiteracy was high and much was learned visually through pictures, sculptures and the like, as well as from lectures and sermons, the whys and wherefores of belief in superstitions and the comfort of tradition is not recorded.

Even today, the majority of us would not bother noting in our diary why we avoid walking under ladders or salute a lone magpie. It's such a familiar part of our culture that it needs no explanation. Yet, why do we do these things? Do we believe, even subconsciously, that something bad will happen if we don't, or have such actions become so engrained in our cultural psyche as to almost be a Jungian folk memory?

How, then, can we begin to interrogate the early modern psyche and glean some meaning from the marks people left on their churches? We can start by looking at events such as the English Reformation, when Henry VIII appointed himself Head of the Church in England and broke from Rome in order to marry Anne Boleyn. Protestantism had, for some time, been vociferously arguing against certain aspects of Catholic practice as superstition, such as transubstantiation (the moment in the Mass when the bread and wine becomes the body and blood of Jesus), praying to statues of saints and belief in relics. During the Reformation, transubstantiation was removed from the Mass, and churches were stripped of their art, relics and statues. Walls were whitewashed, rood screens were torn down and books were destroyed. Yet even without statues, paintings and other images to act as a focal point for the congregation's prayers, belief in them and in their powers persisted. People simply found other ways in which to express those beliefs.

The Church has always had an interesting relationship with magic and superstition, whether it involves an act more commonly known as a 'miracle' or the tradition of priests blessing a plough to ensure a good harvest. There are numerous stories about 'conjuring parsons', which demonstrate that the line between magic and religion has always been somewhat blurred. For example, Parson Joe, from Devon in south-west England, recorded in a notebook the astrological calculations he would undertake on behalf of his parishioners. The Church might have frowned upon the practice, but this particular clergyman believed that it was part of the responsibility he had in caring for his flock.

Others, such as Reverend William Cunningham and Reverend Franke Parker, possessed libraries of 'magical' tomes and had significant local reputations for their occult abilities. Parson Parker, it is said, once left his church partway through a sermon in order to prevent a member of his household staff from reading one of his books, thus averting some unfortunate magic-related incident. It is also claimed that a visitor discovered him in bed on one occasion, surrounded by dead toads. Toads feature prominently in witch lore in England's south-westerly counties.

Parson Parker was also said to be able to shapeshift, a rumour that he seems to have perpetuated himself by claiming that after his death, he would return in animal form. Such was the strength of belief in his ability that when he passed away in the 1880s, his grave was dug twice as deep as usual to prevent the claim becoming reality.[2]

Another Devon clergyman, Parson Harris of Hennock, has an interesting story attached to his magical abilities. Harris was known throughout his parish for his skill in identifying thieves by means of divination, although there is evidence that suggests that, in some cases, psychology proved a more effective tool than anything otherworldly. However, one incident attributed to him clearly demonstrates the conflict between his role as parson and his magical abilities.

One Saturday, Harris asked one of his maids why she seemed unhappy and discovered that she was missing her boyfriend, who had gone into service in Exeter. Keen to cheer her up, Harris told her that he would conjure her boyfriend back to Hennock. However, Sunday came and went with no sign of the young man. The maid went to bed even more unhappy and doubting the parson's skills.

The household was awakened just before dawn the following morning when the maid discovered her exhausted boyfriend outside. After removing his coat the previous evening, he had suddenly been compelled to make his way, overnight and on foot, to Hennock. On today's roads, this is a journey of around 11 miles.

It turned out that his Bible was in one of his pockets, and this countered Harris's working until such time as the young man took off his coat.[3] However, if this is the case, and the Bible really did delay the effects of Harris's working in this way, why did the young man not make the journey to Hennock on the Saturday evening? Did he sleep in his jacket (complete with Bible) that night? The source does not state when Harris undertook his working; perhaps he did not do anything until Sunday morning. Yet, in spite of this issue, the story has survived and been passed down through generations. It seems to have done little or nothing to detract from Harris's formidable reputation.

These stories, and others like them, are anecdotal, yet they serve to illustrate the blurring of religion and magic even among the clergy itself. We see tales of clergymen consulting wise women, accusing people of witchcraft and generally promoting the very beliefs the Church sought so strongly to quash. It is hardly surprising that such beliefs endured through the centuries when the men entrusted with turning their flocks away from such superstition were themselves practitioners and believers. In fact, one even went so far as to permit an unusual artefact to be hung in his church.

On the wall in St Mary's Church, Winfarthing in Norfolk, England, there used to hang an artefact known as the Sword of Winfarthing. It is said that it once belonged to a knight, who killed another knight during an argument over a woman. The knight then sought refuge in the church. Long after he was gone, his sword remained in the church and eventually had so many powers associated with it that it attained the status of a relic. The story explains that if a woman wanted to get rid of her abusive husband, she needed to light a candle and pray before the sword every Sunday for a year. The sword was also petitioned for assistance in finding lost items.

In a time where women were chattels and had no personal agency, independence or legal status, the concept behind this sword is extremely unusual and gives rise to a number of questions. Did it raise eyebrows, or was it accepted more for its powers of locating lost items? How did the women manage to accomplish the act of praying and lighting a candle without being observed by their husbands? And, perhaps most significantly, was this magic, or was it a prayer?

One symbol that has on occasion been discovered in medieval churches, and which never fails to arouse horror when found in such a context, is the pentagram. Known today for its association with 'black magic', it is automatically assumed that its presence in a church indicates that some sort of dark ritual has been undertaken. However, this is not necessarily the case.

As with many symbols, the pentagram has been appropriated and its original meaning forgotten. In early modern times, it was a protective Christian symbol, which can sometimes be found in art being positioned above or on a demon, pinning it down with its points and thereby destroying its power. One example of this can be found in St Mary's Church in Troston, East Anglia, in the form of a graffito on the chancel arch. The profile of a demon's head has been lightly etched into the stone, with a deeply carved pentagram right in its centre. When the image features with humans, however, it is shown beside them, rather than above. In the tale of Gawain and the Green Knight, we note that Gawain's red shield features a golden pentagram known as the 'symbol of Solomon', which gave the prophet power over demons. It is also

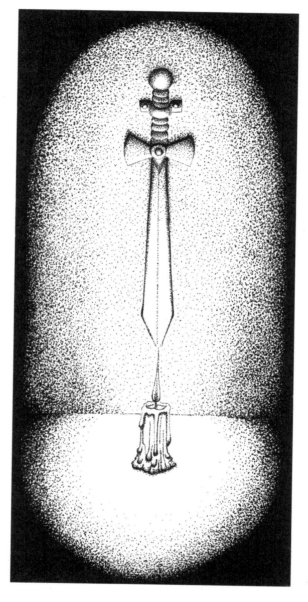

Sword of Winfarthing. (Illustration by Kathryn Avent)

known as the 'endless knot', signifying fidelity, and in the early modern Church, was representative of Christ's five wounds. In Gawain's case, it represented five skills he possessed in which he outshone other knights.

It is, perhaps, surprising to learn that early modern people inscribed curses into the stone of their churches. Like the appearance of the pentagram, this is something with which modern sensibilities are uncomfortable because of its association with dark magic. However, the Bible itself contains curses, which can be found in Deuteronomy 28, a long list of terrible outcomes for failing to follow the Ten Commandments. Verse 20, for example, states, 'The Lord shall send upon thee cursing, vexation, and rebuke, in all that thou settest thine hand unto for to do, until thou be destroyed, and until thou perish quickly; because of the wickedness of thy doings, whereby thou hast forsaken me.'[4]

This does not sound so very different from reports of curses levelled at neighbours by those believed to be witches. When going door to door seeking charity, the poorer members of a community were vulnerable to the whims and individual circumstances of those from whom they begged. On occasion, their requests for aid came at the wrong time and resulted in refusal, leading to angry exchanges and, potentially, accusations of witchcraft later on. Thomas (1971) discusses the outcome of these encounters, which sound very similar to the consequences hinted at in Deuteronomy:

> ... thereafter her cow yielded nothing but blood and water ...
> ... only to find himself unable to make cheese until Michaelmas ...
> ... her little son became sick ...
> ... only to incur the loss of twenty hogs ...[5]

These misfortunes all befell people who had refused charity to women whom they later accused of bewitching them. The loss of twenty animals could well have represented the financial ruin of a farmer; the illness of a child would most certainly cause vexation. Should we, therefore, be surprised to find such curses in any early modern context when communities would have heard them preached from the pulpit and been familiar with them?

The curses found in Deuteronomy made it quite clear that God would destroy you if you strayed from the teachings of the Church, so it is easy to draw a parallel with the smaller-scale act of refusing charity to a neighbour that goes against those very lessons. Thomas states, 'In all cases, denial was quickly followed by retribution, and the punishment often fitted the crime.'[6]

This is rather a sweeping generalisation, and another instance in which psychology probably plays a role. Having knowingly acted in an unchristian manner, it is reasonable to believe that those people would have been hyper-alert to anything that might signify retribution for their actions. If they had refused to give a neighbour some milk or butter, it stands to reason that they would look particularly for problems in their dairy or in their livestock. If such hyper-vigilance led to distraction, it is possible that the person concerned might, without realising, do something that ultimately becomes a self-fulfilling prophecy, such as omitting a step in the production of cheese or butter. Of course, this would not have been the case in every instance of charity refusal, but it clearly happened often enough to make it easy for the misfortune to be linked to the person who had been turned away.

Far from indicating a disrespect to the Church, or a mindset fixated on witchcraft or dark magic, the act of carving a curse into the stonework of a church may, in fact, suggest the opposite. Perhaps the permanence of a carving, in the early modern mindset, was a way to increase the potency of the desire being expressed, an alternative way of calling upon God's intercession.

Of course, it would be wrong to imagine that everything in a church and its associated graveyard can easily be explained away by the early modern mindset or by appropriated symbolism. That is not the case at all. There are numerous instances of illicit acts occurring in and around churchyards, many of which are automatically ascribed to witches, devil-worshippers and other followers of dark magic.

This is a deeply rooted stereotypical view that took hold during the 'satanic panic' of the 1980s; speak to a modern-day practitioner of traditional magic and it quickly becomes evident that they treat places such as graveyards with deep respect. When undertaking a working of any kind within a graveyard, their first act is to silently acknowledge the spiritual guardians of the place and assure them that no harm will be done, and that their purpose is a sacred one. Thus, we see the old religion and the new still inextricably interwoven, still converging at the same places, and those places being treated with the same respect by all believers, regardless of which path they follow.

In medieval magic, north is the direction associated with Satan, and as fonts tend to be sited near the north door of a church, there is often an assumption that the two are connected. Some believe that the font's position enables the Devil to make a quick getaway after he has been exorcised from a newly baptised person, while others believe that the symbolism relates more to one's journey into the church, crossing the threshold of the porch into the church proper and moving closer to God, or the altar, physically as well as spiritually.

Practitioners of traditional magic believe that the liminality of graveyards is a source of great power, particularly those that mark the centre of an extensive network of corpse roads. These were the ancient routes via which coffins were transported for burial and often involved a journey of some miles. There is a fine example of such a route on Dartmoor, known as the Lych Way. This trackway was used by moorland residents from the 1200s onwards, not only for taking loved ones on their final journey to the parish church at Lydford, but also for visiting the stannary court.

The journey was incredibly arduous for those who lived at the far edges of the parish, who petitioned the bishop in the 1200s, requesting permission to bury their deceased in the church at Widecombe-in-the-Moor, which was much closer. Permission was granted for those residents, but in later years, people residing in new dwellings within Lydford parish found that the dispensation did not apply to them, and they were obliged to make the difficult, lengthy trek across the moor to Lydford.

The slopes of Yar Tor are home to a poignant reminder of this tradition, the Coffin Stone. This is a large slab of granite on which the coffin was placed while the bearers took a well-earned rest. The Coffin Stone is now split in two, and has an explanatory legend attached to it. The story tells of the funeral procession of an unpleasant and unpopular man, which had just reached the stone and laid the coffin upon it. Almost immediately, a bolt of lightning struck, splitting the stone in half and consuming both corpse and coffin in the ensuing flames. It was believed that this was a sign from God, preventing such a terrible man from being buried in consecrated ground.

Until the Reformation, graveyard earth appears to have shared the qualities we would ordinarily ascribe to holy water, and this was a widespread belief, not one confined to those who practised traditional arts. When sprinkled across a doorway, graveyard earth was believed to protect a property from harm, and it was also thrown at spirits to make them disappear, in much the same way as we see holy water being used against vampires in any number of movies and TV series. Both graveyard earth and holy water are consecrated, so this use is perhaps not as surprising as it might first appear.

Some acts are, of course, deliberate desecration, such as those carried out in connection with the communion wafer. One Cambridgeshire church has an associated seventeenth-century story of a man who stole a communion wafer and was later caught urinating against the side of the church, holding the wafer in his hand. He had, it seems, been told that if he did this, a toad would appear and eat the wafer, after which the man would be endowed with the powers of a witch. However, various parts of churches have always been used for traditions or activities that fall outside those usually expected in such places. There are, for example, several old traditions surrounding the church porch.

In times past, weddings were undertaken in the church porch. That is, weddings for the common folk. Only the wealthy were able to enter the building itself and marry at the altar. The priest would stand at the door, with the happy couple before him. As well as being a physical threshold into the church, the porch can also be interpreted as a liminal place, between the secular and the holy, between the inside and the outdoors. Perhaps this is why it has become the focal point for so many non-Christian traditions.

Alongside this, we find such rituals as the one carried out on St Mark's Eve (24 April). One would stand in the church porch on that night, and, it is said, would see the 'ghosts' of those in the parish who were soon to die, walking from the church into the graveyard and settling into the locations of their future graves. It was said by some that once a person had undertaken this ritual, they were doomed to repeat it every year thereafter. The price of such curiosity was the burden of knowing who in one's community would die that year, although it could surely be argued that that was the reason for undertaking the ritual in the first place.

In early modern times, people did not appear to be as scared by ghosts as we are today. Their view of ghosts was rather different and centred around the belief that they only appeared if the living had failed to properly undertake their duties towards those who had departed. Right those wrongs and the departed would once again rest peacefully. However, a variety of soothing resolutions to spiritual issues were deemed 'superstitious' during the Reformation and were removed. After this, it seems that ghosts became more of an issue because there was no alternative way to placate them and help them find peace.

Exorcism was one such 'superstition' that was culled under the Reformation, leaving those affected with no recourse to assistance except, ultimately, via the court. Along with numerous other factors, this contributed to the rise in witchcraft accusations passing through the criminal court during the sixteenth and seventeenth centuries. This situation might go some way to explaining why graveyards became places where monsters lurk alongside the restless dead and vengeful spirits.

Knowing that there is a solution to an issue reduces its sting. Thus, it is reasonable to presume that when the safety net of a church-sanctioned resolution was removed, people grew decidedly more uncomfortable about the restless dead. Yet that discomfort has always been with us, to some degree, as demonstrated by what are known as deviant burials. These are burials that deviate from what might be termed 'normal' in such a way as to offer suggestions as to how that person related to their society. Many pre-date the Reformation by thousands of years, such as Iron Age bog bodies.

The most well-known methods of deviant burial are probably the vampiric burial, where a corpse is staked, or otherwise pinned down in its grave, and burial at a crossroads, which may or may not feature staking or other preventative measures. As well as stakings, we see corpses that have been buried face down, or with stones in their mouths. All of these are fairly typical of the methods used to keep the dead in their graves and prevent them from rising to bother the living – or, perhaps, in a Christian context, to keep them from rising on Judgement Day, as punishment for some severe transgression. Likewise, if the stories about Parson Harris are to be believed, then his extra-deep grave can be classed as a deviant burial.

However, not all bodies rose from the grave of their own accord. Some had help from what were known as 'resurrection men' or grave robbers. The most well-known names linked to bodysnatching are probably those of Burke and Hare, in spite of the fact that they were not actually grave robbers.

In the early nineteenth-century Edinburgh, in Scotland, was a leading light in the field of anatomy, but those working in the field at that time kept encountering a shortage of corpses to dissect. This was partly due to Scottish law, which stated that only certain corpses could be used for dissection, such as those of people who had died in prison. This shortage gave rise to an increase in grave robbing that, in turn, led to more stringent measures to ensure graves were protected from such violation.

After the death of a lodger in his house, Hare sought advice from Burke as to what do to with the body, which resulted in the decision to sell it to anatomy lecturer Robert Knox. Knox was, by all accounts, a popular teacher with many students and thus the shortage of corpses hit him hard. Burke and Hare delivered the lodger's corpse to Knox's dissecting rooms and were paid £7 10s, triggering a series of sixteen murders. Knox bought all sixteen cadavers.

Burke and Hare were eventually caught after around ten months. Hare gave King's evidence and was granted immunity from prosecution, leaving Burke to stand trial alone. He was sentenced to death and dissection and his skeleton is now on display in Edinburgh University's Anatomical Museum. Although Knox was not prosecuted, his involvement with the case tarnished his reputation and left its mark for the rest of his life.

Yet while Burke and Hare were not what we might term 'true' body snatchers, preferring murder to the more physically arduous task of digging up graves, others spent hours in graveyards exhuming corpses. This gave rise to several preventative measures in graveyards, some of which can still be seen today.

While walls can be made higher and thus more difficult to scale, the general assumption seems to have been that people would still have managed to breach them. Thus, we see items such as the mortsafes found protecting Scottish graves. These were iron cages that were fitted over a new grave. They were often complicated and secured by two or more keys. From an anatomist's point of view, the fresher the corpse, the better; ideally, it would only have been beneath the earth for a couple of days before being exhumed. Mortsafes tended to be left in place for around six weeks, after which a corpse would be no use to an anatomist. The mortsafe could then be removed and reused. Similarly, mortstones – large, often rectangular slabs of stone – could be placed on top of a grave to prevent anyone digging down into it, again, for a period of around six weeks.

However, these devices were only available to those who could afford them, and such reassurances were not available to poor families. Instead, they placed items such as flowers on the grave to see if there was any indication of disturbance. This would certainly have helped to indicate that a grave had been tampered with, while sadly doing absolutely nothing to prevent such disturbance from occurring. People sat in overnight vigil around their loved ones' graves to deter resurrectionists. Watch houses began to appear, small shelters in which people would sit during the hours of darkness to watch over the graveyard, and an increasing number of vaults and mausoleums began to appear as people sought more and more innovative and secure ways in which to protect their dead and to thwart the grave robbers.

One of the most impressive structures built around a grave may have had a rather different purpose. In the small Devon town of Buckfastleigh, the ruins of the Holy Trinity Church sit atop a hill. The church has suffered a string of misfortunes: arson attacks, grave robbing, vandalism and lightning strikes, to name but a few. It was destroyed by suspected arson in 1992 and since then has developed a reputation as a site of satanic rituals and hauntings, with a long-standing reputation for strange occurrences.

These are perhaps linked to the occupant of a singular grave standing near the church door to the south of the building. At first glance, its purpose is unclear. It is square, with a pyramidal roof. A stout wooden door allows access, and one side has a viewing window covered with substantial decorative metal railings. It may seem unprepossessing, but this building has two interesting aspects. It is one of the earliest mausoleums to be built in England, and it is linked to an extremely dark character.

This is the tomb of Richard Cabell. Cabell, a local squire who died somewhere between 1672 and 1678, is said to be the inspiration for Black Hugo in Sir Arthur Conan Doyle's famous Sherlock Holmes story *The Hound of the Baskervilles*.

Cabell certainly had an appalling reputation. It was claimed that he had murdered his wife Elizabeth Fowell, and made a pact with the Devil, stories that have persisted to the present day. It is said that if you run around the tomb seven times and then put a hand through the iron bars, either Cabell or the Devil will bite your fingers. Local people have reported seeing strange lights near the tomb, while others claim to have seen demonic figures around it. On the anniversary of his death, Cabell is said to lead the Wild Hunt across nearby Dartmoor. All these stories have combined to conjure up an image of a truly unpleasant and evil man, resulting in the structure over his tomb being seen not as a method to keep grave robbers out, but to keep Cabell in.

As with many such legends, it is impossible to pinpoint with any degree of accuracy whether it is partially true, or a complete fabrication. A quick online search for Elizabeth Fowell Cabell reveals that she died in 1686, thus outliving her husband by some years. Cabell may have been unpleasant and not well liked in his community, as the legend states, but it seems that whatever else he may have done to inspire a character such as Black Hugo, murdering his wife was not one of those deeds.

Another common, yet mysterious image within medieval churches is that of the Green Man, a term coined in 1939 by Lady Raglan in her article on the subject for *Folklore* journal. Most often seen as a carved boss in church ceilings, the Green Man is also more properly known as a 'foliate head'. Typically, humanoid facial features are depicted, the eyes and mouth disgorging a variety of leaves. Oak and ivy are frequently seen, but given the character's close links to the natural world, such representations may be seen with almost any foliage and may feature trees, flowers and fruit based on the seasons. The majority appear to be male, but there are also some Green Women.

Depictions of foliate heads in churches are often explained away as representative of old pagan traditions that were superseded by Christian rites. They represent fresh growth and the cycle of life, so their main association is with the spring, but in more recent years, they have come to symbolise the environment as a whole. Representations such as Dead Papa Toothwort in Max Porter's novella, *Lanny* (2019), illustrate this shifting viewpoint by depicting the shapeshifting 'green man' moving through the landscape, sometimes as an insect, sometimes as a piece of litter, sometimes as a plant. Dead Papa Toothwort hears, sees and *is* everything around him, demonstrating the interconnectedness of everything we see in our environment, from the mightiest tree in the forest to the ephemera with which humans litter the world in the name of progress. Given the close relationship our ancestors had with the land, where life and death hinged on the state of the harvest, it is possible that representations such as Porter's would, perhaps, be quite familiar to them.

The earliest examples of foliate heads date back to Roman times and are found across the world, but since Lady Raglan's article, parallels have been drawn with figures such as the folkloric Jack-in-the-Green, the Arthurian Green Knight and the god Pan. She also likened them to the flower-bedecked Garland King character who features in the Derbyshire town of Castleton's Garland Day pageant, which coincides with Oak Apple Day on

Green Man. (Illustration by Kathryn Avent)

29 May.[7] As this type of calendar custom is seeing a resurgence in Britain, Green Man figures costumed in large, elaborate arrangements of tatters and flowers are seen more frequently and are becoming more familiar.

The oldest foliate heads in Britain tend to date from around the twelfth century, which gives rise to the question of which came first, the characters or the carvings? The origins of Jack-in-the-Green are unclear, although there is a suggestion that he developed from the ever more elaborate flower garlands in sixteenth-century May Day celebrations, which ultimately became a full costume and an individual entity in its own right. Yet the story of Gawain and the Green Knight dates from the fourteenth century, with the Green Knight clearly a metaphor for the cycle of growth, death and rebirth with which contemporary audiences would have been deeply attuned, both in their relationship with the land they worked and in the sermons they heard in church. Thus, we can see that the concept of Jack-in-the-Green is of significant age, even if the character itself is somewhat more recent.

The Green Man is sometimes associated with Herne the Hunter and the Horned God and thus has, over the centuries, become entwined with the Wild Hunt. This is a term first used by the German writer Jacob Grimm in the nineteenth century to describe a spectral chase, led by a central figure. There are stories of hunt leaders such as Odin, King Arthur, the Devil, Herne the Hunter, and our unpleasant Devonshire squire, Richard Cabell.

The Wild Hunt is a riot of demons, spirits, black goats and ghostly black hounds, an image straight from hell that is guaranteed to strike terror into anyone unfortunate enough to witness it. Such victims were commonly thought to be carried off to the faery realm or the underworld, never to be seen again.

Why, then, do we find so many foliate heads in medieval churches, looking down at us through their leaves, berries and flowers? Is it, as the popular theory states, linking the pagan past with the Christian present, or is its significance more secular? Given that priests often blessed ploughs or fields to ensure a good harvest, it is reasonable to presume that foliate heads fell into the category of 'acceptable superstition', and their inclusion in prominent places within the church was the community's way of acknowledging not only their dependence on nature and their environment, but also on the interconnectedness of all things.

In her book *Traditional Witchcraft: A Cornish Book of Ways* (2008), Gemma Gary explores the close relationship between religious belief and belief in traditional magic and healing. She describes some of the charms produced by a traditional practitioner, known as a pellar, who lived in Helston, Cornwall in the nineteenth century. The pellar used graveyard earth, teeth, bones or charms inscribed on small squares of paper, all of which were intended to be enclosed in tiny bags and worn round the neck as a preventative against ailments caused by bewitching, such as fits. Some of the charms, Gary explains, were for extremely religious clients, who tended to choose a significant verse from the Bible to carry with them and seem to have been an intercession to God for the pellar's healing to succeed.[8]

It was not only Bible quotes that traditional practitioners employed in their workings, however. This was a time when the Church influenced every aspect of life for everyone, from birth through to death and beyond. While it might be surprising to learn that many of the charms employed by traditional healers in the south-west of England featured prayers and psalms, when seen in the context of the Church's dominance over everyday life, it becomes more understandable that there would be some crossover between the divine and secular. Gemma Gary's *The Black Toad* (2011) discusses preventative methods against the ill influence of a black witch, one of which involves salt, which can be scattered around the place or person affected, while the other employs Psalm 68. This psalm, which begins, 'Let God arise, let his enemies be scattered: let them also that hate him flee before him' can be used, Gary explains, by both client and practitioner either during a working or while making preventative charms.[9]

Folklorist Ruth St Leger Gordon recorded numerous charms gathered from her neighbours on Dartmoor in Devon. These, too, indicate a close association between religion and more traditional beliefs and practices, for each one contains some degree of religious imagery and language, sometimes referencing Bible stories or biblical characters and tending to end very much in the style of a prayer with the words used when making the sign of the cross: 'In the name of the Father, and of the Son, and of the Holy Ghost, Amen'. Charms for staunching the flow of blood from a wound often reference Jesus stilling the waters of the River Jordan, while various toothache charms feature a conversation between Jesus and the toothache-afflicted disciple, Peter.

St Leger Gordon spent some considerable time collating and recording the charms either being used in the Dartmoor community or remembered by them. She has, without doubt, preserved a significant amount of material that would otherwise have been lost, yet her attitude towards some of the material she recorded is rather scathing and dismissive, as can be seen in her assessment of several charms, including this one for 'burn-gout' (original spelling used), which dates back to at least 1899 and which she found in the *Transactions of the Devonshire Association* for that year:

> Three or four fair maidens came from divers lands crying for burn-gout – acheing, smarting and all kinds of burn-gout – they went to the burrow town – there they had brethren three – they went to the salt seas and they never more returned again – he or she shall have their health again in the name of the Father, the Son and the Holy Ghost.[10]

'The words of these charms cannot be considered as anything but crude gibberish to which a Biblical veneer has been applied,' St Leger Gordon states.[11]

Taking the charm above at face value, she does have a point. Salt is believed to have protective attributes, which might explain its presence here, but the rest of the wording makes little sense. I do not think it should simply be dismissed, however. This is a charm that has been actively used at some point during history, indicating that it was believed to have the power to either cure or ease the symptoms of this type of joint pain, which is caused by an excess of uric acid in the blood.

The blend of religious and secular wording we see in this charm does not differ significantly from what we see in the case of the Sword of Winfarthing, or in the symbolism of a foliate head. All three successfully meld aspects of religion with more traditional beliefs to produce something new that held great significance for their respective communities. The fact that our modern sensibilities do not understand the symbolism or its significance should not detract from its value as an insight into how our ancestors viewed the relationship between the sacred and the mundane. It should also be borne in mind that they likely did not consciously differentiate between the two, seeing them simply as facets of a single, overarching belief system.

Bible extracts have been used as amulets since the beginnings of Christianity, and the use of amulets generally has seen repeated attempts to both suppress and promote it at various times over the centuries. Amulets are held to possess power in their own right, whereas an amulet from a mainstream religion generally needs to be blessed or consecrated in some way to become endowed with similar attributes. The conflict between religion and traditional magical practices has thus been a contentious issue since the advent of Christianity, with numerous writers in antiquity condemning a variety of practices, including wearing the Scripture as an amulet. The implication of such a criticism appears to be to question the strength of the faith of anyone who needs a physical item to bolster it. However, it could easily be argued that a rosary provides the same kind of comfort that would be derived from a religious amulet, albeit in a slightly different context, as the rosary is primarily an aid to prayer. Yet is touching a piece of paper with a significant biblical verse any different from touching a rosary?

It should by now be apparent that magic and religion did not diverge and follow two entirely separate paths following the introduction of Christianity. Rather, they entwined, each taking on aspects of the other. For example, Christianity adapted numerous existing festivals and days of significance, drawing them into its calendar, while we see a crossover of religious imagery entering the realm of the amulet, particularly the image of the cross. This symbol was linked to Christianity from around the second century CE, but was not particularly widely used, perhaps due to the negative connotations of what it represented – an instrument of death. Eventually, however, use of the cross extended until, in the sign of the cross, it became a prayer in and of itself. Over the centuries, it has been the one image that has become synonymous with Christianity, except during the English Reformation in the sixteenth century, when performing the sign of the cross was deemed a symbol of papacy and therefore something that should be excised from the new Church of England.

We see amulets in many religions and many countries. In Egypt, amulets were crafted in bone and the finely glazed ceramic known as faience, as well as materials such as metal, stone and gold. The most common were the ankh, which symbolised eternal life, and the Eye of Horus. This was a stylised eye with an eyebrow above and a long curling tail extending from the lower lid and was comprised of lines and symbols that represented thought and the five senses. The oldest amulets are believed to be those discovered in Egypt's Pre-Dynastic Badarian culture, dating back some 4,000 years and depicting hippos and antelope. Coptic Christians had written amulets, usually containing quotes from the Gospels, the Lord's Prayer or Psalm 91.

In Palestine and Syria, the most popular type of amulet was crafted in thin, flat sheets of copper, lead, silver and gold. Quotations, incantations and references to God would be cut into the metal with a needle, then the item would be rolled up and stored in a metal container, which could be worn as a necklace. China similarly favoured written inscriptions, creating a system of calligraphy that they believed would provide protection against evil spirits.

We also find written inscriptions in Jewish amulets, as the use of symbolic amulets, such as the hippos and antelopes favoured by the Badarian culture, would have been viewed as idolatrous. In Judaism, amulets can be made from any material and be any colour. Those details are unimportant; the only thing of significance is the name or words contained in the inscription. Two of the most famous amulets are the Silver Scrolls, dating back to the sixth or seventh century BCE and featuring extracts from the text of the Priestly Blessing from the Book of Numbers.

Interestingly, another familiar amulet from this region is the Hamsa, or the Hand of Miriam, also known as the Hand of Fatima. It symbolises the Hand of God and has protective qualities, as well as being a good luck charm. Unusually, this is not a written amulet, but a symbolic one. It is shaped like a hand, fingers pointing downwards, and can be plain or extremely ornate, often with a circular or eye-shaped detail in the palm. This symbol is seen in several different religions, including Christianity, where it is known as the Hand of Mary and undertakes a similar protective function.

There is a type of Muslim amulet traditionally believed to cure hiccups in children and which causes controversy, as it is viewed as going against Islam. This is the hazaazah. Money is collected from seven people named Muhammad and is taken to a blacksmith, who creates the amulet, which is then pinned to the child's clothes.[12] It is seen as *shirk*, the sin of polytheism or idolatry, and is thus *haraam*, or forbidden, in the Islam faith.

A popular amulet in the Christian faith is the medal of St Benedict. Its exact age is unknown, but it has been an approved aspect of the Catholic faith since the mid-eighteenth century. The Order of St Benedict's website details the many uses of these medals, one of which is to place it in the foundations of a house for protection.[13] Given that there are numerous instances of items such as shoes being placed in foundations, beneath thresholds and hearthstones and up chimneys for the same purpose, we see here the line between magic and religion becoming increasingly blurred. There is ostensibly no difference between these two acts except for the fact that one of the items is deemed to have significance within the state-sanctioned religion of the day, while the other is not.

If someone wished to afford their home such protection today, however, they would need to purchase a mass-produced medal (a wide variety are available online). We have already seen that such items do not possess power in and of themselves; it is only when blessed by a priest that they take on special significance. The medal would, therefore, need to be blessed before being placed into the foundations. Yet the shoe, when used as an apotropaic charm, is imbued with those powers without any need for additional rites or ceremonies to be pronounced over them.

In traditional rites and rituals, there might be a particular instruction or condition that needs to be fulfilled for the item to be imbued with its powers, such as being gathered at midnight under a full moon or having previously belonged to a person from a particular sex. In such a context, these conditions could be interpreted as a form of blessing, or, conversely, the blessing could be considered a condition to be fulfilled to confer power upon an item. Again, the main difference between the two appears to be that one has the approval of the state-sanctioned religion, while the other does not.

The medieval Church inherited a view of magic from the belief systems of antiquity and thus we see a continuation of the school of thought which held that amulets were demonic in nature – except for the cross. Over time, there has been a definite shift away from the melding of religious and traditional imagery in amulets and towards purely ecclesiastical iconography and shape. More recent centuries have seen a marked increase in the number of cruciform amulets, while other previously popular shapes are seen less frequently. In fact, in Western Christianity, amulets generally are seen only rarely until around the eighth and ninth centuries, with grave goods tending to feature more traditional decorations such as floral imagery.

Yet, in spite of the Church's continued condemnation of amulets, there are numerous examples of members of the clergy producing such items, particularly in times when low literacy levels meant that monks or priests were some of the only people who possessed the necessary knowledge and skill to be able to do so. Even the saints were described as producing amulets, which were imbued with power relating to those with which the saint was particularly associated.

The line between magic and religion, between miracle and magic spell has always been blurred, and although there does seem to have been a definite shift towards Christian iconography in amulets, as opposed to traditional, their use has frequently been condemned as idolatrous. Yet in many cases, all that separates a religious amulet from a traditional charm is the user's belief that the power in the item originates from God. Given the number of examples of traditional charms that invoke God's aid, however, this distinction is not as clear cut as one might expect, and it does seem to depend largely on the individual's personal viewpoint and the depth of their interaction with either an amulet or a charm. The two cannot even be categorised according to the depth of an individual's faith, for those favouring traditional methods are frequently as deeply religious as those who cleave solely to more conventional religious prophylactics.

One of the most unusual images to be seen in a medieval church is the sheela-na-gig. This is a bald female grotesque that can mainly be found throughout the United Kingdom. They are not limited to churches, being located also on walls in non-religious buildings. They are generally naked and sit with splayed legs, holding open their vulva with both hands. Some, such as the well-known example on the exterior of Kilpeck Church in Hertfordshire, England, have large, stylised eyes and noses and a somewhat enigmatic expression.

Their origins are unclear. They seem to date from the twelfth to the sixteenth century, although some scholars believe that they may be considerably older and, perhaps, influenced by European grotesques. Even their name remains enigmatic, as there does not seem to be any etymological origin for it. Much disagreement has arisen over aspects of the name, with some suggesting that it refers to breasts, and others to female genitalia. Some sheelas do feature breasts, but in most examples none are evident, with all the attention being focused on the vulva.

In Ireland, there is a belief that some women were called sheela-na-gigs and would expose themselves in order to ward off the evil eye, perhaps harking back to the belief in phallic imagery as apotropaic. There are stories from across the world featuring women driving off some form of evil by exposing their genitalia. However, the story of the Greek goddess Demeter demonstrates that this was also a gesture relating, as one might expect, to fertility. After losing her daughter Persephone to the underworld, Demeter mourned for months, during which time the earth was barren. Only after a woman named Baubo raised her skirt to display her genitalia to the goddess did Demeter leave off mourning, allowing the world to become fertile once again. Similarly, in Irish folklore, we find the tale of Queen Medb, at war and outnumbered, exposing her genitalia to her enemies on the battlefield, resulting in them retreating in confusion.

What, then, can we deduce about the nature of the sheela? Is she a fertility goddess or charm? Is she a warning against the perceived evil of female sexuality? Or is she an apotropaic talisman of sorts, with numerous applications? There are certainly stories and arguments favouring each, as well as more recent interpretations, such as that by Gimbutas (1999) in which the sheela is seen as a toad goddess.[14]

This moves interpretation some distance away from schools of thought that view sheelas as part of a targeted ecclesiastical campaign against immorality. Could this campaign be a form of appropriation of the tale of Queen Medb, taking the act of 'skirt raising' and applying a rather more negative interpretation? Medb's act was one of power and positivity, ultimately driving off her enemies and maintaining the safety and stability of her lands and her people. For the church to steer male congregants away from immorality, however, it is necessary to shift the opinion of 'skirt raising' from a positive and apotropaic action to the misogynistic and stereotypical 'beware the evil of women', in line with the Bible's presentation of female sexuality as inherently evil.

Yet the placement of sheelas within the church building itself suggests that this interpretation may not be strictly accurate, as some are located over a doorway and thus can be seen in their apotropaic form, protecting the building itself from evil influences. A curious example of this can be found in the porch of St Mary the Virgin Church in Chipping Norton, Oxfordshire, England. The two-storey porch is itself unusual, being one of just three hexagonal porches to be found in English churches. Its vaulted ceiling is decorated with carved stone bosses, including a green man, but there is also a carving described as a sheep overpowering a wolf.

The carving is oval. The sheep's head is directly above the wolf's and its limbs reach round on either side of the carving, essentially forming the oval and framing the two heads, with its anthropomorphic hands appearing to be pulling the wolf's jaws apart. However, aspects of the jaws and the position of the hands on either side of them, echo the various depictions of the vulva of sheela-na-gigs. Is this carving really of a sheep and a wolf, or was it once a sheela that has been reworked in later centuries to accommodate more delicate sensibilities?

The carving seems to be less worn at the top of the boss than at the bottom, and there are some interesting stylistic differences. The sheep's fleece is carved in a similar manner to the hair on a human head and a lion's mane in two other bosses, but it is far less detailed, being more representative than those around it,

Ceiling boss in the porch of St Mary the Virgin Church, Chipping Norton, Oxfordshire. Sheep and wolf, or repurposed sheela-na-gig? (Photo ©James Shakeshaft)

Ceiling boss in the porch of St Mary the Virgin Church, Chipping Norton, Oxfordshire. (Photo ©James Shakeshaft)

which feature individual carved locks. Its eyes, too, are simpler and slightly different stylistically to the eyes in the other bosses. The sheep's 'arms' appear to be wearing sleeves, with shaping at the wrist reminiscent of a cuff, and the shoulders are extremely robust. By contrast, the wolf is virtually featureless, consisting mainly of a hairless head with large eyes and no apparent ears. The nose is shaped oddly; its position coincides with what would be the top of the vulva in a sheela, so the nose and snout are bizarrely indented, reminiscent of teeth on a jack o'lantern, rather than convex, as we might expect in a representation of a wolf.

The Victorians removed several sheelas; is this one that survived because it was able to be disguised as something else? If the interpretation is correct and the figures are of a sheep and a wolf, perhaps this particular image was chosen to represent false prophets, the wolf in sheep's clothing mentioned in Matthew 7:15. In this context, the image in its current state could be interpreted either as a straightforward representation of a wolf wearing a fleece, or as a member of the flock of Jesus, represented by the sheep, overcoming a false prophet in the shape of the wolf.

The meaning of the imagery has been lost to us over the centuries, and little more may be gleaned by looking at those who created them. Did the stonemasons receive specific instructions from those commissioning them, or was their reputation and the quality of their work such that they were given a degree of free rein in the designs they produced? Were they even British, or were they Norman stonemasons, used to more exhibitionist bosses and carvings found in some European churches, particularly in Spain and France? Were they simply taking a familiar feature and introducing it into a new location?

The fact that sheelas appeared in churches at all indicates that, like graffiti and the various other unusual features we have examined, there was a time when their inclusion in the decoration of a church was entirely appropriate, or at least, not so offensive as to warrant removal. The message they were intended to convey was, in all probability, one that could have been decoded at a glance by a congregation skilled in such interpretation.

The power ascribed to churches and churchyards, regardless of which religious path one follows, is such that it has been drawn

Devonshire Toad Magic. (Illustration by Kathryn Avent)

upon in traditional charms to destroy the power of black witches. In her book *Silent as the Trees* (2017), Gemma Gary describes a fascinating working involving toad magic, a popular feature of traditional practice in England's south-westerly counties.

For this ritual, one must gather three stone jars, three frog livers and three toad hearts. The livers must be stuck full of new pins and the hearts with thorns from a holy thorn bush. One of each is put into each of the stone jars. The practitioner then visits three different graveyards and buries one jar in the path of each, at a certain depth and at a proscribed distance from the church porch. It was believed that anyone undertaking this ritual was thereafter immune from the evil influence of witches.[15]

As we have seen, some of the imagery and iconography we see today in medieval churches is not what it first appears. It is not vandalism as we know it, nor is it desecration. Rather, it is the remnant of a rich and complicated relationship between tradition and religion, and between Christianity and other religious paths, each borrowing at times from the other with the ultimate aim of requesting something from, thanking or otherwise petitioning a higher power. Despite the tantalising physical record they have left behind, the nuances of our ancestors' decoding of the imagery in their churches will, very likely, always be beyond our grasp.

REFERENCES

1   Champion, M., *Medieval Graffiti: The Lost Voices of England's Churches* (London: Ebury Press, 2015).
2   Gary, G., *Silent as the Trees* (London: Troy Books Publishing, 2017).
3   *Ibid.*
4   The King James Bible (London: Eyre and Spottiswoode Limited).
5   Thomas, K., *Religion and the Decline of Magic* (London: Penguin Books Ltd, 1971).
6   *Ibid.*
7   Raglan, Lady, 'The "Green Man" in Church Architecture', *Folklore*, Vol. 50, Issue 1 (1939).
8   Gary, G., *Traditional Witchcraft: A Cornish Book of Ways* (London: Troy Books Publishing, 2008).
9   Gary, G., *The Black Toad* (London: Troy Books Publishing, 2011).
10 St Leger Gordon, R.E., *The Witchcraft and Folklore of Dartmoor* (Newton Abbot: Peninsula Press Ltd, 1994).
11 *Ibid.*
12 Norman, M., *Telling the Bees and Other Customs* (Cheltenham: The History Press, 2020).
13 'The Order of Saint Benedict: The Medal of Saint Benedict', www.osb.org//gen/medal.html (accessed 25 January 2021).
14 Rhoades, G., 'Decoding the Sheela-Na-Gig', *Feminist Formations*, Vol. 22, No. 2 (2010).
15 Gary, G., *Silent as the Trees* (London: Troy Books Publishing, 2017).

Athenodorus and the Ghost. (Illustration by Kathryn Avent)

3

FOLK GHOSTS

When we examine stories of ghosts within folklore, we should be mindful that they are split at the broadest level into two distinct categories: alleged sightings and folk ghosts. In the former case, reports will exist with details that may be investigated (names, dates or third-party involvement, for example). The incident may not have happened in the very recent past, but it has not yet been consigned to history. It is the latter category that is more generally the sphere of the folklorist.

Of course, like many things in life and most in folklore, it is rarely that clear cut. We are used to the motif of the liminal boundary in many forms within folklore; that state where edges are indistinct, and things are neither one nor the other. The same state exists within stories of ghosts and spirits.

Accounts of hauntings that purport to have a basis in truth go back a long way into the historical record. Distinct from the stories in Classical Greek literature, for example, which have their roots firmly in the cultural mythology of the region, Pliny the Younger recorded a haunting in a house in Athens in the first century AD:

In the dead of night, a noise was frequently heard resembling the clashing of iron which, if you listened carefully, sounded like the rattling of chains. The noise would seem to be a distance away, but it would start coming closer ... and closer ... and closer.

Immediately after this, a spectre would appear in the form of an old man, emaciated and squalid, with bristling hair and a long beard, and rattling the chains on his hands and feet as he moved.[1]

The residents of the house were so plagued by the ghost that they eventually left, and the building became impossible to find tenants for. After some time, a philosopher named Athenodorus, who was newly arrived in Athens, came across the house, which had been put up for sale at a very low price. Although told the reason for the bargain, he was still happy enough to make a purchase and moved in.

Considering himself to be a rational and intelligent man, Athenodorus did not believe the stories as recorded by Pliny. Until one night, that is, when the rattling of chains heralded the arrival of the same spirit. The apparition beckoned the philosopher to follow it, which, in his own time, the man did. He was led out of the house and into the courtyard, at which point the ghost vanished.

The following day, having left a marker the night before, Athenodorus requested that the spot was excavated. Buried under the courtyard, the skeleton of a man in chains was discovered. It was obviously significantly aged as the bones were not only stripped of any flesh but had also been corroded by the irons. A proper public burial was conducted for the unknown man and after this time the spirit never again appeared in the house.

This account, and others of a similar time, raise various difficulties because of their age. The original sightings were recorded as true at the time, but many centuries later the boundaries have become somewhat indistinct and what started as eyewitness accounts have taken on far more of the attributes that would normally be ascribed to a folk ghost.

What exactly *is* a folk ghost? To answer that question successfully we first need to consider what makes a ghost in folklore terms.

We may think that the answer to this question is quite straight-forward; a ghost is the apparition of a previously living being. In fact, the composition of the symbol to which we ascribe the term 'ghost' is rather more fluid than this, due in part to the fact that our understanding of any symbol may vary by time or place.

In folk-based stories the ghost often replaces an earlier motif that exhibited similar characteristics. David Clarke, for example, notes that in texts from medieval England, people were afraid of revenants – creatures that would emerge from their grave at night spreading disease and death as they roamed abroad – but in later times the ghost had replaced the undead as the source of the fear. Beliefs in the destructive elements continued, however, along similar lines.[2]

The same is true of fairies, who seem to have a new role within folklore as the antiquated scapegoat for events that we interpret differently today. The similarities between fairy reports and UFO abduction accounts are well established and I have discussed them in my book *Black Dog Folklore*.[3] Professor Owen Davies, working along similar lines, makes the point that it was belief in fairies or other such sprites that may often be used to explain an event in a certain geographical place that is classed as a 'haunting'.[4]

There is, of course, no definitive story that lays out the origins of fairies. One of the older possible alternatives is that they are the souls of deceased persons who have been trapped on earth in some kind of limbo state. (We may take limbo as a word deriving from the Latin '*limbus*', which translates as 'edge'. Thus, aside from the theological interpretation of a border between the next worlds of Heaven or Hell, we come back to the earlier concept of more general liminal boundaries within folk beliefs.)

This is an argument that was proposed by Scottish clergy-man and antiquarian Reverend Robert Kirk. He wrote the text *The Secret Commonwealth of Elves, Fauns and Fairies* in 1691 but the book was not committed to print until the nineteenth century, at which time the well-known folklorist Andrew Lang published a copy including his own comments and endnotes. Kirk begins his first chapter, entitled 'Of the Subterranean Inhabitants' with the words, 'These Siths, or Fairies, they call Sleagh Maith, or the Good People, it would seem, to prevent the Dint of their ill attempts ... and are said to be of a middle nature betwixt Man and Angel, as were Daemons thought to be of old.'[5]

Scholar of Devon folklore Theo Brown (1914–93) made a similar suggestion about fairies being the remnants of lost prehistoric races in her book *Devon Ghosts*.[6] This is of less use to us in this discussion, however, than her work in the book *The Fate of the Dead*, where she makes several observations on folk ghosts.

Brown acknowledges the dividing of ghost accounts into the two categories of those alleging to be true and those that are legend-based but notes that the folklore which connects the two plays a crucial role. The latter folk ghosts will often have an impossible aspect to their character that is not found in the simpler haunting accounts. The ghost of Sir Francis Drake, for instance, is said to drive across the wilds of Dartmoor at night atop a black hearse that is drawn by four headless horses. The cortege is accompanied by dogs, which are similarly headless, and running devils.

There are several aspects to this ghost that obviously signify it as a folk ghost. Overlooking the fact that, in the manner of other 'celebrity' spirits such as Anne Boleyn, the ghost haunts multiple locations simultaneously, we note the many impossible elements: headless horses or running devils. We should also, where possible, delve into the backstory when we examine ghost accounts to look for origins or other clues.

Sir Francis Drake purchased Buckland Abbey (now owned by the National Trust) in Devon in 1582. He undertook extensive building and renovation works to the property. According to stories in the local area, these only took three nights to finish because Drake had made some form of deal with the Devil. Here we find, therefore,

Buckland Abbey. (Photo © Tracey Norman)

the spirit appearing as a condemnation motif. Retribution in death is a common signifier of a folk ghost.

The fact that Drake is a well-known figure also places this ghost into the legendary category. We find both of the last two points highlighted in Theo Brown's work, where she identifies four key aspects to the folk ghost. The first of these we have already noted; that is that there are no first-hand accounts of experiences of these spirits. The stories come from written records or oral retellings.

Secondly, folk ghosts are based on the memory of a person who actually existed and, in most cases, can be identified by name. With many of these legendary hauntings the person involved stands out over others from their community because they have some sense of power about them. This may have been monetary in nature; it may have been because they were particularly unpleasant in character, or it may have been that they were intellectually powerful. Often in these stories the trade of the person draws them out as having been above others in their community. Examples may include weavers, tailors or inventors.

Whatever the reason, the innate abilities that the person had caused them to stand above the masses. The population inevitably became hostile towards them, either because of their actions or through jealousy. Alongside this, however, they were too formidable to tackle head on in life and so it was after they had died that vengeance was sought against them.

Although the ghosts of these characters would usually appear in their own guise, in other examples classed as folk ghosts they take the form of animals.

The final common aspect identified was that the hauntings are rarely benign when dealing with folk ghosts. In these stories, the peace of the community is usually broken by the spirit. This should not really appear surprising when we consider the second point above, with everyone else becoming hostile against the character involved. A powerful figure would most likely want to exact some form of revenge for all of the jealousy or character assassination against them, rather than sitting back and letting it wash over them. The ongoing disruption leads to a religious leader or scholar having to banish the spirit to restore normality, either by consigning it to a remote area or by other means. The methods of banishment have commonalities within folklore, and we will move on to these shortly.

By way of illustration, we might take the story of a weaver named Knowles, who lived in the hamlet of Dean Combe situated in an area of the south-west of the United Kingdom known for its cloth manufacture. Knowles was said to be one of the best weavers in the area, consistently producing the finest knap. Because of his skills, Knowles became a rich man but was not very generous with his wealth. Alongside this, he was hated by his neighbours, who said that he was an evil, selfish gossip.

Knowles worked from sunrise to sunset each day, eventually dying while sat at his loom in the loft. Despite being disliked in the parish, many local residents came to the man's funeral. This was more to wish well to the weaver's son Fernley than it was to the old man. Fernley was a much more pleasant and respected man in the parish, and he knew that he would now have to prove that he had the skills that his father had taught him at the loom.

The day following the funeral, Fernley knew that he must start work and so descended to the kitchen to light the fires and take some breakfast before beginning. While sitting at the table, Fernley was shocked to hear the familiar sound of the loom thumping upstairs in the loft. He crept up the stairs to investigate, thinking that perhaps someone had broken into the house. Easing the door slightly ajar and peering round, however, a rather different sight met his eyes. There at the loom sat the ghost of his father, the old weaver, working as ever he had done.

Alarmed and confused, Fernley could think of nothing to do but fetch the local vicar, who came to the house, thinking that he would need to employ the traditional bell, book and candle. Arriving at the house, the vicar remained on the ground floor and shouted up to the weaver to leave the property and return to his proper place in his grave.

'I will as soon as I have finished this quill!' cried out the spirit of Knowles in an unearthly voice.

The priest again commanded the spirit to leave the house and return to the graveyard. This time the spirit came downstairs, at which point the priest threw holy water into its face while reciting a prayer. With a scream, the image of the weaver transformed into a ghostly black dog. Through use of the Bible the priest brought the dog to heel and commanded it to follow him, where he led it down the lane to the local woods. Here the priest banished the spirit to a task. Picking up an acorn shell by an oak tree, the priest told the dog form of Knowles that he would find eternal rest only when he had emptied the pool in the woods using the acorn shell. Legend still says that the local moorland people will not visit the pool at either noon or midnight because they will see the image of the

Knowles the Weaver in dog form. (Illustration by Kathryn Avent)

terrible black dog trying desperately to empty the pool with the acorn shell so that it can find its rest.

This story very neatly draws together many of the key aspects of folk ghosts that we have already discussed (the hated figure, the skilled individual and the impossible aspects for instance), as well as other common motifs within folklore. The mention of noon and midnight as the times at which local people would not visit the pool should be of no surprise. These are liminal times; the boundaries between states where the time is neither one thing nor the other. It is not morning, nor afternoon, not a.m. or p.m. These transitory times are always significant in folk beliefs.

The story ends with the spirit of the weaver being banished to a task that must be completed before it can be laid to full rest. This idea comes up with many folk ghosts. Because, as we have already seen, these spirits are often people who have been unpleasant or evil in life, this task is used to symbolise retribution for their deeds.

It is part of the use of the folk tale as morality teaching that we see often when examining folk stories. Many of these morality aspects come from the Christianisation of older tales and the Church's use of them to teach right (the way of the Church) from wrong (everything else). This does not imply, of course, that the modern Church is to blame for this. It is important to remember that stories and beliefs change and develop all the time as they travel and are adopted and adapted. It is all part of the natural cultural shift. It has gone on for thousands of years and it will continue to do so.

In the tale of Knowles the weaver, as in many others, we can see this in action as the spirit is commanded and controlled by the priest through the use of prayer and the word of God, in the form of the Bible. This is the symbol of evil being banished by good.

At this point, it is probably useful to clarify exactly what the idea of the banished ghost refers to. In modern times, if a person or a place are believed to be troubled by a ghost (or sometimes a demon, particularly within the views of the Catholic Church in Westernised cultures) then a rite may be undertaken to try and remove the spirit. This is often done by a priest who has undergone specialist training, although other laypersons can and do profess to do the same. We know this rite as exorcism.

Exorcism is not undertaken lightly, particularly in the Church, and can be extremely dangerous. This is because whatever you may personally believe might be being dealt with, an individual's own beliefs, psychology and mental state are being tapped into. From time to time, tragic cases are reported in the media where individuals have died during exorcism. These come from various cultures and countries. Belief in possession is highlighted as a potential danger in some child protection guidelines, so it is taken very seriously.

In previous centuries, the word 'exorcise' was not used to describe ghosts being contained or banished. In written accounts from earlier times, we read of ghosts being 'laid down'. This term connotes more that the spirit is being put to rest rather than being driven away. The procedure would always follow a set pattern.

Folklorist Theo Brown, once again, in her book *The Fate of the Dead*, provides an interesting description of this.[7] She notes that a minister would always be called in to perform this task. There are two main variants to the procedure. One of these is the banishment and the other is the trapping of the spirit in a suitable receptacle. In the case of the latter, an unquiet spirit is being secured to prevent it from causing further trouble to people. The minister would be asked to read the spirit down and then, by candlelight, he would recite passages from the Bible. This would cause the ghost to be diminished in size, bit by bit, until it was small enough that it could be contained in a bottle or a box. This might then be buried, placed in a tree or a chimney, or possibly thrown into a pool. Common periods of time are often cited for the containment of the spirit – sixty-six or ninety-nine years – which seem like odd numbers until you consider that thirty-three years was generally classed as a generation.

One obvious use of tales such as these is to prevent people from doing something that you do not wish them to do. In the same manner that smugglers invented ghosts to keep people away from their illicit activities (an idea we will come back to shortly), legends of an unruly ghost that might be released upon the digging of a field or the draining of a pool would have a similar effect. If you look for them, there are lots of places in the landscape that are said to cause ill fortune if interfered with. Examination of the origin stories will often throw up many similarities.

And such is the nature of folk ghosts. There are many recurring themes and happenings ascribed to multiple characters. Unlike pure historical accounts that take place at a definite location A, in folklore a reported event at location A may have variously also happened in a similar way at B, C, D and E. This is not to say, however, that folklore studies are distinct from history, as some academic historians argue. Folklore should rather, in my opinion, be viewed as a subset in the Venn diagram of history and social studies. Folklore and tradition are born from historical facts in many and various ways, making it a part of any country's cultural history. This makes it ideally suited for adoption by fiction authors. After all, folklore was originally an oral tradition and so the art of storytelling is vitally important here.

It would serve us well, for the remainder of this chapter, to examine three different types of folk ghost that may be illustrated by comparison to the folklore record. Between them they have several stories reflecting the themes to which we have paid some attention thus far. It should then become apparent how these motifs and similarities present themselves, which will help to train the eye when examining stories found through the reader's own research or investigation.

COCKSTRIDE GHOSTS

The first of the two variations of laying down a spirit that we examined, the banishment to an impossible task, provides the root of the cockstride ghost. The tasks to which unquiet spirits are banished are always impossible to complete – weaving ropes from sand, picking single blades of grass to clear an area or emptying a pool with a receptacle with a hole in it. The implication is that the spirit will be bound until Domesday, in the same way that trapping a spirit in a box prevents them causing more trouble. Where a ghost is banished rather than being contained it is allowed to return to its home, or to the site of its original haunting, at the rate of one cockstride each year.

The book *A Dictionary of English Folklore* tells us that a cockstride was a country term for a tiny distance and was used to describe the increase in daylight in early January.[8] For example, in John Ray's 1678 collection of proverbs, 'At twelf-day the days are lengthened a cock-stride'.[9]

Writers have drawn upon folklore over the centuries through the 'tale within a tale' literary device. One who uses this mechanism in our field of study is Thomas Hardy, whose combined literary works give a valuable insight into the customs and beliefs of rural areas in the past. Both Hardy's poetry and prose are littered with pieces of folklore and tradition, although for the most part these are frustratingly brief.

As he was raised in rural Dorset in the mid-nineteenth-century, Hardy would have been exposed to many elements of traditional lore, aspects of rural life and stories that are of particular interest to folklorists today. Many of these he used in his narrative tales and poetry as plot drivers, but their inclusion does much to idealise the Victorian landscape and those characters who Hardy placed within it.

The ghost and haunting motifs employed by Hardy particularly tend to appear as folk ghosts in distinction to 'actual' apparitional hauntings. Folklorist and Hardy scholar Peter Robson has noted that although many of Hardy's ghosts are drawn from his own imagination, they still behave in the manner of traditional ghosts. In other words, Hardy was taking existing beliefs and traditions about ghosts and haunting folklore and mapping these onto characters or spirits of his own invention. Hence, the 'tale within a tale' literary device.

In *The Woodlanders* we have the tale of two brothers who haunt Kings Hintock Court. They are exorcised by a priest but return to the court at the pace of a rooster every New Year's Day. This is accounted for by the local saying, 'On New Year's tide, a cock's stride'.

Local folk tales can provide writers with a narrative of past events that are then presented conversationally within the story. It is unclear exactly where Hardy found the inspiration for this particular tale, although it possibly comes from one of the Cornish stories. There are multifarious stories of the ghost-laying successes of Parson William Wood of Ladock, who was rector of the area between 1704 and 1749. This is one character who may have been drawn upon.

>⊷⊶⊙⊷⊶≺

In her 1996 presidential address to the Folklore Society, Jacqueline Simpson, speaking about ghosts in M.R. James's writings, points out that in Denmark cockstride ghosts are malevolent whereas British ones are penitential.[10] As we have already noted, this does not mean that there was generally anything pleasant about the person involved when they were living.

Sir John Popham was Speaker of the House of Commons from 1580 to 1583 and subsequently served as Attorney General and Lord Chief Justice. He presided over the trials of Sir Walter Raleigh and Guy Fawkes and was evidently not the sort of fine, upstanding citizen that you would expect of someone in these positions of authority. He is rumoured to have secured the ownership of Littlecote House in Wiltshire by condoning a horrible crime perpetrated by his kinsman, Wild Will Darrell. In old age, Popham retired to his native Somerset and built a house for himself in Wellington. His wife, who was a rather more pious character, predeceased him.

The Popham family tomb is at Wellington Church, but it is said that Sir John Popham is not buried there. According to local legend, he got his comeuppance for his controversial life when he was thrown from his horse into a deep ravine in the Blackdown Hills. The location became known as Popham's Pit in memory of this event.

Legends say that the pit is bottomless. This is a common motif often ascribed to pits as well as other natural holes such as ponds. In the case of the latter, this story would be used in the way that folklore so often is, as a way of keeping people away (so that they did not fall in and drown). As far as pits go, the idea of them being bottomless is usually connected originally with the suggestion that they are an entrance to the underworld.

The story tells that Sir John Popham died horribly and descended into Hell. However, on account of his wife's prayers for him, it is said that his spirit may rise on New Year's Eve and move back towards the church at a cockstride, not being able to rest in peace until it gets there.

Two points in this story should immediately mark themselves out to the observant student of folklore. One is the recurrence once again of the calendrical date of New Year's Eve as the time at which the spirit may rise. The second is the fact that it is because of the intercession of his good, Christian wife that he may be saved. Many folk tales have been used for, or adopted as, morality lessons.

Another legend attached to this story tells that there are tunnels leading from the sides of the pit. One of these is supposed to link with the family tomb at the church and it is along this passage that he is said to be able to crawl. There is a farm lying on the line of this route and early in the nineteenth century strange noises were heard under the floor of the house. A white witch (to use the old-fashioned terminology of the story) was brought in and, realising that the noises were caused by Popham's spirit, he banished him back to the pit once again.

The tunnel leading from one significant point in a story to another is a common element of many folk tales. These are almost always apocryphal and even a cursory examination of the topography of an area on a good map will often prove why. In the case of Popham's spirit, for example, the pit is some 3 miles away from the tomb.

Another cockstride ghost that fits firmly into the folk ghost requirements we have already established is that of Jack Radford, a Victorian hunting parson whose grave may be found in the village of Lapford in north Devon. Radford died in 1861 and became the focus of several horrific legends. He was renowned as a womaniser. It was remembered clearly that he allowed his hounds to terrorise the children of the village and some people believed that he hanged his own curate. The parson desired to be buried in the chancel of his church when he died but the villagers would not stand for this and buried him in a grave outside the north wall of the church – this area would have been reserved for unbaptised children, people of poor character and, later, those who had committed suicide.

It is possible that this prejudice against burials to the north comes from an idea that is common in apocryphal literature that Hell lay to the north. This is why we find in many traditional types of play that the layout of the stage is carefully configured so that heaven is in the east, with good characters entering from the south and west and bad characters, as a rule, from the north. The idea carries forward into pantomime, where villains will always enter from one side and the hero or heroes from the other. There has also been a suggestion made that the idea has its root in the Bible itself, in the book of Jeremiah, Chapter 6, Verse 1, where it states, 'Evil appeareth out of the north'. We saw this with regards to church architecture in the previous chapter.

Because of this and the fact that Radford did not get his wish with regards to the location of his burial, his spirit is said to be discontent. A small hole can sometimes be seen in the grave through which he may pass and try to return to the Old Rectory, at the pace of a cockstride. The legend also says that the stone cross of the grave will not remain upright. This part at least is true: the cross used to be cemented upright and when I visited it was also secured by a metal plate running down the back of the stone and into the wall. It is probable, of course, that ground subsidence causes this, but the effect feeds naturally into the legend and adds credence. Ironically, Jack Radford's grave marker is now the only one that stands vertically in a field of slewed and toppled headstones.

The author R.D. Blackmore who, like Thomas Hardy, often used local characters and stories in his works, adopted the parson under the name of Rambone in his book *The Maid of Sker*. Blackmore, however, described him as a nicer person than the original. This goes further to demonstrate that there is often some crossover between local lore and fiction with authors who set their pieces in their own locale.

In the wonderfully named village of Coffinswell, an unnamed lady is buried for reasons unknown, but no doubt sinful, beside the village's holy well rather than in the consecrated ground of the churchyard. Her story is useful to highlight the real-world logical flaws in the motif of the cockstride ghost. Once a year (and again at midnight on New Year's Eve), she is permitted to rise and try to gain the churchyard at the rate of a cockstride.

The woman's story was recorded by the Reverend Sabine Baring-Gould towards the end of the nineteenth century. It is said that it will take until Judgement Day to reach her destination, but as usual, she will find salvation when she gets there. It is interesting that the motif is strong enough that the story lives on in this case even though the name of the protagonist is lost.

How does this case highlight the improbable nature of many of these legends? If we think about it carefully, we must assume that if she will eventually reach her destination and so gain salvation, then she is progressing along a path. Each year she rises from her grave to take her cockstride. So, what is happening to the grave? Is it moving with her and if so, why has nobody noticed? Or does she get some free distance each year, so that after ten years she rises from her grave and gets ten free cockstrides before her allotted one?

One final example of a cockstride ghost provides an interesting variation to the folklore, where the pattern of events runs in reverse – in other words, the travel at the rate of a cockstride comes first, with the laying down by the parson occurring at the end of the tale. The event is listed as having been written down, or recorded in some way, by John Bastone, a dairyman baptised on 30 March 1817.[11] Although it seems irrelevant, that date information is useful to help us to place the account in time from its first few words. He said:

About 120 years ago, the ghost of a Mr Lyde appeared in the orchard on the east side of the road running along the foot of Salcombe Hill.

Every year the ghost advanced a cock-stride nearer to Sid House, until, at last, it sat on a gate on the opposite side of the road.

Then, still at the incredibly slow pace of a cock-stride each year, he proceeded to an old oak tree almost in the centre of the field. This oak tree, although a bit battered by the storms of many years, is still to be seen standing in the meadow.

After many more years, the determined spectre arrived in the cellar of Sid House. A maid-servant, on going to the cellar to fetch liquor, saw the ghost of Mr Lyde sitting on a barrel, eating bread and cheese, with a quart of cider beside him. Eventually, to the horror and dismay of the people living in the house, the ghost, with a look of triumph, sat down to dinner with them one night.

The family decided that to share their table during their evening meal with an apparition was more than they could bear, so one of them rode to Mr George Cornish of Pascombe in the Harcombe Valley, to ask him if he would come and try to lay the obstinate ghost.

Mr Cornish arrived, carrying with him a small Bible, and with very little difficulty laid the spectre.

Although that appears to be the account as originally recalled, some interesting extra detail was compiled in the 1920s by local historian J.Y. Anderson-Morshead when putting together archives of the parish. In these it is noted that when the ghost reached the gate, six ministers were called to lay him but could not. So why should Mr Cornish have found it so easy when the other six failed?

The answer is said to lie in his education, which took place at Oxford. It is generally stated in folklore of this type that only an Oxford scholar can lay a bad ghost and so presumably the other ministers were not educated there.

This account also adds a postscript to the story that reminds us of the tradition of reading ghosts into a box for burial or similar. The day after Lyde's spirit was laid, they drove a donkey cart to a local field with his possessions and laid him with gravel for fifty years in a pit.

The Lydes are an old family in the area and the most likely original for this ghost is Thomas Lyde, who died in 1824 and is buried in the family vault in Sidmouth Parish Church. His dates match Reverend George Cornish, who served the area between 1821 and 1828 before moving to Cornwall. This means that John Bastone would have only been a child at the time and so we must assume he is relating gossip rather than providing an eyewitness account.

Further reports of this ghost being seen certainly exist in 1870 and 1920, and there is a suggestion that he was still around as late as 1979. This is an unusually recent date for a haunting story of this type, but still sits comfortably within the category of folk ghost as there is no eyewitness account and only scant detail.

We have already noted that cockstride ghosts tend to be penitential and so the reason for the haunting is most likely guilt. Lyde is rumoured to have murdered his uncle and there is also a tradition of some form of treasure buried under an elm tree. To die leaving wealth hidden was seen as an injustice to your heirs and hence the spirits of anyone who did so were unlikely to find easy rest.

PHANTOM COACHES

In 1921, Victor Sjöström released the film *The Phantom Carriage*, a ghost story. It is not a particularly well-known film today but it is more influential than you may realise. Not only did the film go some way towards advancing the career of Ingmar Bergman, but it also featured one scene that would become iconic when represented in another later film.

David Holm, the central character of the story, appears in one scene hammering on a locked door, behind which his wife and children hide. After a short time, he begins hacking at the door with an axe. Most people would never realise that the famous scene in Stanley Kubrick's 1980 film *The Shining* was not an original concept.

The main premise of the storyline of *The Phantom Carriage* ties together neatly the motifs of the cockstride ghost with those of the ghostly coach, a staple of folk ghost symbolism. The plot is constructed around a legend that the last soul to die on New Year's Eve (that boundary date once again) must collect the souls of the dead for the following twelve months and see them to their place of rest.

David Holm is a drunk and he dies on the stroke of midnight (another important time in folklore tales). He is shown his past life in an attempt to get him to change his ways and protect those around him. The parallels with Charles Dickens' *A Christmas Carol* should be obvious – another example of the use of folk ghost symbolism in literature as a mechanism of morality.

We may return to the works of Thomas Hardy to find what is probably the best-known example of a phantom coach in literature, that of the D'Urberville family in the novel *Tess of the D'Urbervilles*, which follows a common pattern for motifs of this kind. An ancestor of the family commits a terrible crime, there is a phantom coach containing his spirit that is seen in the generations that follow and it is a portent of ill omen to see it. In the novel, Angel Clare describes the story briefly to Tess:

> 'Oh – you have heard the legend of the d'Urberville Coach – that well-known superstition of this county about your family when they were very popular here; and this lumbering old thing reminds you of it.'
>
> 'I have never heard of it to my knowledge,' said she. 'What is the legend – may I know it?'
>
> 'Well – I would rather not tell it in detail just now. A certain d'Urberville of the sixteenth or seventeenth century committed a dreadful crime in his family coach; and since that time members of the family see or hear the old coach whenever – But I'll tell you another day – it is rather gloomy. Evidently some dim knowledge of it has been brought back to your mind by the sight of this venerable caravan.'
>
> 'I don't remember hearing it before,' she murmured. 'Is it when we are going to die, Angel, that members of my family see it, or is it when we have committed a crime?'[12]

Usually the portent applies to anybody, but in some cases, such as this one, the phantom is visible only to members of the family. Family ghosts and portents are not uncommon. Often, they apply to black dogs or other animals, but in other cases a different symbol is attributed to the legend.

As with much of his folklore, Hardy's legend is based on an existing story. He draws on the phantom coach of the Turbervilles, which follows a very similar theme, although the details of the legend have become rather mixed. In *Thomas Hardy's Dorset*, first published in 1922, Robert Hopkins cites a wicked Turberville whose life of drinking and vice sent him into temporary madness. He murders a friend while they are riding in the coach to Woolbridge House. Hopkins states that the phantom coach and horses runs the road from Wool to Bere with the murderer in pursuit, but never catching up.

A later version of the story puts the events in the reign of James I and says that John Turberville eloped in a carriage and four with Lady Howard, the daughter of Viscount Bindon. The spectral coach drives from Wool Bridge House to Bindon Abbey. Some, but not all reports, mention that you can only see the coach if you have Turberville blood.

Phantom coach stories are relatively common, and the main themes are frequently replicated across them. They are, despite this, not a particularly well-studied motif in many ways and an in-depth analysis is probably long overdue. The Folklore Society requested a survey of them in 1938 and the results were published in the pages of the journal *Folklore* in 1942.[13] This paper recorded around sixty examples across the United Kingdom, with a significant number in the West Country and five in Dorset, including the Turberville coach. This is, of course, just the tip of a very large iceberg. Edward Waring presented a paper entitled *The Phantom Coach in the West Country* at a folklore colloquium at the University of Exeter in 1971 and had collected eighteen carriages in Dorset at this time. My own research has identified more than that number in the county.

Waring noted that several of the records have the coach ending its journey by plunging into water or a marsh. He believed that this stemmed from a pre-Christian belief regarding a wagon collecting souls; an idea drawn on by the Swedish film with which this section began. Folklorist Christina Hole suggested that phantom coaches may be an evolution of the belief in the Wild Hunt, which was extensive across north-west Europe during the medieval period. Witnessing the Wild Hunt was also said to portend misfortune.

In fact, many coaches probably have no distinct identity at all and are just tragic motifs. As we have already discussed, it is the nature of folk ghosts that many of the stories are very vague in their origins. It is easy to see that there are parallels between the occupant of a ghostly carriage offering a lift, with the associated threat of some portent or ill fortune, and the image of the Wild Hunt. We are essentially dealing in many cases with a psychopompic vehicle – a conductor of souls, as Waring reasoned.

Sometimes, the spirit in the coach is an erring human being condemned to drive between two points as retribution for their sins. Jacqueline Simpson and Jennifer Westwood note in *The Lore of the Land* that where coaches are not anonymous they are usually attached to landed proprietors against whom there is some kind of grudge.[14] These two points categorise these tales very firmly into the same subset as many of the cockstride ghosts in the previous section, as well as the overarching folk ghost more generally.

One particularly well-known phantom coach story is that concerning Lady Mary Howard of Tavistock. She was the daughter of Sir John Fitz and was a rich heiress who married four times. Each time she married she added significantly to her wealth. Lady Howard was orphaned at the age of 9 when her father committed suicide. He had become extremely rich by inheritance at the age of 21 and this had led him on a moral slide. He was a very unpopular character in the town and ended up murdering two men at the doorway to his house during a fight, one of whom was his best friend.

After Sir John's death, King James I intervened in the family affairs and sold Lady Mary to the Earl of Northumberland. The earl forced her to marry his brother, Sir Alan Percy, when she was 12. Much of Lady Mary's life continued to be equally tragic. Only one of her four husbands was actually married for love, and he died after an illness. But because of the hatred shown towards her late father by everyone in the town, she began to be disliked by proxy.

All the elements of a tragic story leading to the creation of a folk ghost are evident.

Even though the criminal in this story was really her late father, the animosity towards Lady Howard is very apparent. With her father gone, the wronged parishioners had to turn to his surviving daughter to vent their displeasure. The events of her own life gradually became merged with Sir John Fitz's and after her death the stories of her husbands' deaths became more and more malicious. Even though there was, and is, no evidence to suggest that Lady Mary Howard had anything to do with the passing of any of the men, the legend began to develop over time that she had killed them all. And so, with all the criteria fulfilled, Lady Howard took her place as a folk ghost in the history of the area.

It was said that every night at midnight her coach would emerge from the gateway of Fitzford House. On the four corners of the coach were placed the skulls of her four husbands and in front of the vehicle ran a black greyhound with one eye in the middle of its forehead. The ghost of Lady Mary sat inside the coach in one version of the story; in another, it was she who transformed herself into the greyhound.

The story told that if one was walking the route of the coach at night and the vehicle came along, then Lady Mary would stop and offer a lift. Of course, it was prudent to refuse this offer, or a suitably sinister outcome would be sure to follow.

The destination of the coach was the castle in Okehampton, a town approximately 15 miles away from the family seat in Tavistock. Originally built as a motte and bailey castle, the stone keep had been extended into a high-class residence in the fourteenth century and was at one time the largest castle in Devon. The last owner had fallen foul of King Henry VIII in 1538 and by the time of the reign of James I it was empty and would begin to deteriorate into the ruins that remain today.

Okehampton Castle. (Photo © Tracey Norman)

The castle sat atop a grass mound in a wooded spur across the river and this mound provided the site of the penitential task to which the spirit of Lady Mary was said to be doomed. As the coach drew up at the foot of the hill, Mary would descend and pluck a single blade of grass, which she then had to take back to her coach and drive home. She was bound to repeat this task until the whole mound was cleared, signifying of course as with the earlier examples a method of trapping for all time a ghost considered to be a threat.

The story of Lady Mary's phantom coach is one of the earliest examples of the type in Devon, but as with most folk ghost motifs it is not without its problems. Lady Howard died in 1671, but people living in the rural area of her home at this time were unlikely to have known what a carriage even looked like. This is because the roads prior to the introduction of the turnpikes at the beginning

Lady Howard plucking grass. (Illustration by Kathryn Avent)

of the eighteenth century would have been in such poor condition that it would have been impossible to run a carriage on them. It is known, in fact, that Lady Mary did not even own a carriage.

An inventory of her possessions at the time of her death showed that she was the owner of a sedan chair that she used for travel.

The prominent element of the spectral dog in both versions of the story may suggest a possible reason for the way that it developed. Of itself, the dog does not really seem to fit with the history and story of Lady Howard. But in folklore terms, there must be a reason for it to be there. It is not uncommon for more recent ghost stories to be mapped onto older traditions when two stories co-exist in the same area. Sometimes this happens when there is not a clear explanation for the older story, as a way of trying to give it some context. But in other cases, they just naturally merge over a long period of retelling, if they are both on the same road, for example, or in the same building. The route taken by the phantom coach of Mary Howard seems to be paralleled by several 'runs' of black dog hauntings along local roads that were already in the folklore record at the time, and so it is possible that her story has been superimposed onto an older tradition in this way.

When we consider both the stories of Lady Mary Howard of Tavistock and the phantom coach of the Turberville family over the county border in Dorset together, as we have just done, then I am tempted to speculate on whether hers either borrows from, or has been confused with, one of the versions of the Turberville story over the years. At first glance, there do appear to be some similarities. Both stories occur in the reign of King James I. Both concern a daughter called Lady Howard and both mention a wicked male character. Of course, the coach is the folk motif in both.

But this is, we must be clear, only a theoretical starting point. More work (which at the time of writing has not been undertaken) would need to be done in order to try and establish a stronger link. There is no obvious connection with phantom dog folklore in the

Turberville case, nor does there seem to be any kind of penitential task. And why should the story travel from one county to be mapped onto a different piece of folklore? I don't have the answers to these questions at the moment, but it provides an interesting backdrop for speculation.

In similar fashion to Lady Howard, there is a case concerning a Madame Widecombe of Combwich in north Somerset where, if accepting a lift from her, the carriage is said to plunge into the river and vanish in a cloud of steam. This echoes both the warning of not accepting a lift from a phantom coach and the ending of a journey in water as described in Edward Waring's previous research.

><+>•O•<+><

In the nineteenth century, we find several reports of ghostly conveyance in the form of hearses. As well as transporting spirits of the deceased, less ethereal versions of these coaches were also used to transport spirits of a slightly different kind. It has been suggested that many of the stories of ghostly carriages have their roots not in actual historical events, but rather in the imaginations of smugglers. These men would have invented many of these stories in order to keep people away from the areas in which their clandestine business was carried out.

One example of the way in which this was done, using the motif of a phantom coach, may be found in the parish of Kingskerswell in Devon. On the Barton Hall Estate, a tree that became known as the Brandy Bottle Tree was a regular cache for spirits. The goods were conveyed from the coast in a hearse, which was painted with luminous paint and pulled by horses whose hooves had been padded so that they made no sound as they moved. If you imagine that the horses were painted with the same luminous paint, apart from their heads, then the common symbol of the headless horse may also have been created.

Of course, this idea of the constructed ghost creates something of a chicken and egg situation. Did the image draw on a previous existing tradition in order to give it credence to witnesses? If it did not, then how well would it have worked? The passage of time is such that we will never have answers to these questions.

As with many other types of folk ghost, sometimes the phantom coach is not seen at all, but plays out as an auditory experience. There is a well-recorded example of this in the town of Dartmouth. The Royal Castle Hotel is a very old property that is something of a time capsule on the inside, retaining a lot of ancient wood panelling and beams of roughly hewn timber. It has been suggested that these were salvaged from the wood of a wrecked ship from the Spanish Armada.

The phantom coach story at this location is connected to the time of James II. It was in the autumn of 1688 that William and Mary, following James' flight to France during what is now termed the 'Glorious Revolution', came to England from the Netherlands to claim the throne. Mary was the first to arrive, and she lodged at the Royal Castle while she waited for William to follow. At that time, the hotel consisted of two pairs of houses that were separated by a narrow court.

It was William's intention to also land at Dartmouth, but he was diverted during the crossing by a storm in the Channel and he ended up docking at Brixham instead. A coach was duly despatched to collect Mary and it arrived at the Royal Court shortly after 2 a.m. This is the time that its phantom still continues to arrive, according to the legend.

Both staff and guests at the hotel have frequently reported being roused by the sound of horses' hooves clattering over cobblestones. This is followed by the sound of footsteps and then a carriage door being opened and slammed shut. There then comes the crack of a whip, the noise of horses and then the wheels of the coach as it rides off into the night. This event is always said to be marked by the sound of a clock striking two in the street behind the hotel, where no clock exists to account for the noise.

We have already seen that folk ghosts are usually attached to particular locations and naturally, in the case of phantom coaches, these will often be a stretch of road rather than a building. One obscure story from the village of Uplyme, found on the border between the counties of Devon and Dorset, tells that in the year 1970 the witness (a 9-year-old boy at the time) was out cycling with some friends. He had made his way ahead of the others and was out of their sight when he says that he saw something that he described as a stagecoach 'like you see in pictures'. It was red and black, trimmed with gold, and was pulled by a team of four horses. The driver, he said, wore some sort of eye mask and had a cap with a red feather in it. Two other men rode on horses alongside the coach. The witness says that he saw the carriage turn out of a white gate and come straight towards him. He momentarily looked away, but when he looked back it had vanished.

Some of the details of this case seem to tie in with the history of the road, which used to be the old coaching road at Whitty Hill. At the point where the boy says that he saw the coach, it is recorded that there was indeed a pair of white gates that were no longer there in the 1970s. This fact was apparently unknown to the boy at the time, which adds an extra twist to the story.

RITUALS AND REPETITION

This third aspect of the folk ghost motif draws attention to the fact that many of these hauntings appear legendary because of the ways in which they may repeatedly play out. Repetition is, of course, a large part of the ritualistic behaviours we may find in any culture from the smallest gesture, such as a handshake, to the largest annual celebration. In this case, however, the term ritual is used more to imply a calendrical ghost, that is, one that is said to appear on the same date each year and most likely perform the same function.

These calendrical spirits are among the most prevalent of ghost stories. For example, Tommy Golden and Julia Coate note:

> Recurring apparitions are ghosts that occur in regular cycles over a period of time, usually once annually. This type of ghost sighting is one of the most popular. The date of manifestation usually occurs on an anniversary date or a day of special importance to the deceased. These apparitions can include both ghosts of people and animals. Reports of recurring ghosts include individuals who have committed suicide, murder victims, and entire phantom armies marching across battlefields.[15]

The repetition angle of the folk ghost may apply not only to the action of the ghost, but also to recurring stories of a similar nature in different locations. While the authors above correctly note that the recurrence of an apparition is often linked to an important date, additionally, the recurrence of a ghostly motif in different places may also be linked to an important moralistic message. We already know that the use of folklore as a morality tale is one of significant importance. Using the aspects of ghostly people and ghostly animals noted in the quote above, we can demonstrate both of these repetitive elements of the folk ghost.

The murder of Thomas Becket, the Archbishop of Canterbury, in 1170 is well known, particularly as he is seen as a martyr by both the Anglican and Catholic Churches. Becket disagreed with the monarch at the time, Henry II, and was murdered in Canterbury Cathedral by four men who were supporters of the king. Considering his position as archbishop and the position of the Church in the twelfth century within daily life, it is not surprising that much of the folklore surrounding Becket also surrounds religion and the Church in some way, shape or form.

Much of this early folklore is based around the county of Kent. In the Middle Ages, Kent boasted the richest and most popular healing shrine in Britain in that of St Thomas Becket. Chaucer's *Canterbury Tales*, written in the 1380s, follows a group of people heading for this shrine. Becket was claimed to cure every type of disease and the thirteenth-century 'miracle' window in the apse of his cathedral at Canterbury depicts some of the miracula claimed for Becket by the monks who would tend the shrine. We may also find other fascinating folklore relating to Becket in that area, such as the intriguing story of one village that is said to have been cursed by Becket so that children born to its inhabitants came into the world sporting tails.

It is to the apparition of Becket himself, however, that we need to turn to examine the recurring aspects of the folk ghost. The heart of the folklore is not so much the actual murder as finding penance for committing it and it is this that places both Becket and his murderers within the folk ghost trope. Many churches are dedicated to Becket or have stories attached to them of having been built or funded by the men who slew the archbishop. There are obvious concentrations of these around the geographic areas where the men lived, and the provenance of the stories is not always easy (or indeed possible) to prove.

One of the four murderers, William de Tracey, has a large number of churches related to him in some form in this penitential manner. The village church at Lapford in Devon is alleged to have been significantly rebuilt by de Tracey and the building was also rededicated to Becket when a tower, chancel and porch were added. Observant readers will note that this is the same church that we examined earlier when looking at the cockstride ghosts, with reference to Parson Jack Radford.

The ghost of St Thomas is said to ride through the village (and past the church that is now dedicated to him) calendrically each St John's Eve, 27 December. His journey is said to be taking him to meet with William de Tracey at the nearby village of Nymet Tracey.

There are some confusing aspects to this story, which is quite vague in many ways. Because there is no obvious origin to this legend, we cannot say what the motivation of Becket's spirit is to meet with his murderer. There is also no obvious explanation as to why this event is generally recognised as taking place on 27 December, when the anniversary of Becket's murder is actually two days later on 29 December. Although most sources considered to be more academic place the story on the earlier date, this is no guarantee of accuracy when there is insufficient evidence to support the claim.

In an interesting parallel with a similarly repetitious aspect, we find a ghost reported at South Leigh in Oxfordshire at a church that has links to Becket. In this case, the ghost is of an unnamed murderer. The connection with the archbishop comes from the local tradition that one of his murderers went to the church there to obtain absolution, but was refused and rode away. A galloping horse is said to be heard approaching the church and then departing on the anniversary of this event. The story itself, in this case, seems to be rather vague and lacking in detail.

This is, as we have already seen, the nature of the folk ghost. Its story is usually sparse in this way. Nobody really expects to see the ghost of Thomas Becket ride down the street. Especially when not everyone can agree on the correct date for him to do so! Nor does anyone try to explain the illogical aspects of the cockstride ghost motif. And if a phantom coach really does appear regularly at 2 a.m. in a particular location, why have we not proven the existence of ghosts once and for all to the sceptical community?

The answer, of course, is that we are not trying to prove that a folk ghost exists. There is little in most ghost stories of this type to suggest that they represent an actual haunting. What they do represent, however, by their continued inclusion in local history books, travel guides, stately home websites and many other publications, is the continued strength of storytelling and its power of embedding a tale into our social history and culture.

REFERENCES

1 *Pliny*, Book 7, Letter 27: 'Letter to Licinius Sura'. Trans. www.ancientstandard.com
2 Clarke, D., 'Scared to death: fatal encounters with ghosts', *Contemporary Legend*, 3 (2) (2013).
3 Norman, M., *Black Dog Folklore* (Cornwall: Troy Books, 2015).
4 Davies, O., *The Haunted: A Social History of Ghosts* (New York: Palgrave Macmillan, 2009).
5 Kirk, Reverend R. and A. Lang, *The Secret Commonwealth of Elves, Fauns and Fairies* (1893).
6 Brown, T., *Devon Ghosts* (Jarrold Publishing, 1982).
7 Brown, T., *Fate of the Dead: A Study in Folk-Eschatology in the West Country after the Reformation* (Cambridge: Mistletoe Series, 1979).
8 Simpson, J. and S. Roud (eds), *A Dictionary of English Folklore* (Oxford: Oxford University Press, 2003).
9 Ray, J., *A Compleat Collection of English Proverbs: Also the Most Celebrated Proverbs of the Scotch, Italian, French, Spanish, and Other Languages: The Whole Methodically Digested and Illustrated with Annotations, and Proper Explications* (J. Hughs, 1737).
10 Simpson, J., '"The Rules of Folklore" in the Ghost Stories of M.R. James', *Folklore*, 108 (1997).
11 Weinberger, E., *Karmic Traces* (New Directions Publishing, 2000).
12 Hardy, T., *Tess of the D'Urbervilles* (Penguin English Library, 2012).
13 Mrs Cowie, 'Phantom Coaches in England', *Folklore*, 53, No. 4 (1942).
14 Simpson, J. and J. Westwood, *The Lore of the Land: A Guide to England's Legends from Spring-Heeled Jack to the Witches of Warboys* (Penguin, 2006).
15 Golden, T. and J. Coate, 'Ghost Hunting: The Scientific and Metaphysical Approach', lulu.com (2011).

Slenderman. (Illustration by Tiina Lilja)

4

URBAN LEGENDS: THE DARKER SIDE OF STORYTELLING

When I was around 10 years old, a friend told me a terrifying story about a girl and her boyfriend whose car had broken down on a deserted road at night. The boyfriend went off to get help, the girl stayed with the car. After a while, she became worried. A branch was tapping unnervingly on the roof of the car. As the night wore on, the girl's fear and panic increased ... and then she was suddenly surrounded by police cars, lights flashing. She was told to get out of the car and walk straight to the officers, and not to look back. She got out, started walking, and then turned back. On top of the car was a man, holding her boyfriend's head on the end of an axe and tapping the roof of the car with it.

I didn't know it at the time, but that was my first experience of an urban legend. It was told with great earnestness and plausibility and, given that it was late at night, and we were in a tent in a field next to a wood, it contained the perfect amount of spooky realism to scare a group of pre-teen girls. It was entirely convincing; its efficacy is demonstrated by the fact that I can clearly recall its telling, years afterwards.

The Boyfriend's Death. (Illustration by Tiina Lilja)

What marks out a story as an urban legend? Usually, there is something about it that is just too good to be true. The protagonist experiences a form of karma that ties in neatly with the subject of the story, and the stories themselves are too slick – everything in them has a purpose. There is often an element of jumping to conclusions on the part of the protagonist. The main feature of these stories, however, is that they always happen to a friend of a friend. The storyteller is never talking about their personal experience.

Like folkloric legends, there may be variations of these stories, but the core elements remain the same. A good example of this would be the legend of Lady Mary Howard, which has its origins on Dartmoor in Devon, England, and which was discussed in Chapter 3. The version of the 'murdered boyfriend' story, which was told to me, where the crazed killer is sitting on the car roof with the boyfriend's head, is a popular European variation of that tale. In the US version, the boyfriend has been suspended above the car and the girlfriend mistakes the sound of his dripping blood for rain.

One particular urban legend with a number of regional variations involves a holidaying family – parents, children and grandmother. The grandmother passes away in the car as they are heading to their destination, so, as the kids don't want to share the back seat with a corpse, Dad bundles Grandma up in a blanket and puts her on the roof rack. They find the nearest town and stop to ask for advice.

On returning to the car, they find that it has been stolen, along with Grandma. They never recover any of their belongings ... or Grandma. This story is a favourite in Europe, and there are variations in the USA and Australia. Leading expert in urban legends, Jan Harald Brunvand (1999) points out that in the US version, the family is generally travelling in either Canada or Mexico, and they are often towing a boat, in which Grandma is placed before being stolen.[1]

The urban legend I personally have heard most recently is an old one involving an alleged gang initiation ritual, a story that has also been prevalent in the USA for many years. When driving at night, the legend says, if you see a car approaching with its headlights off, you should drive past without reacting. If you flash your lights at the driver to alert them to the issue, you will have marked yourself as the target in the ritual. In order to join the gang, the driver has to murder the occupant of the first car to flash their lights in this way. This urban legend was being circulated on Facebook as a warning to people living in my area. It was presented plausibly and resembled many other 'warning' posts, such as those passing on information about suspected dog thieves operating in a particular town.

Urban legends are transmitted orally in the same manner as folkloric tales, but today, they also form part of the traffic that travels the world via the internet, with the potential to reach a global audience in no time at all. As with folkloric legends, their origins are, for the most part, lost in time, although there are some that can be linked to specific events.

There is one, however, that can be tracked from the moment of its creation, giving folklorists a truly unique insight into how such stories arise, and how they are built on and circulated thereafter. That urban legend is the story of Slenderman.

A great deal has been written on the Slenderman story after its rise to infamy following the tragic incident that took place in Waukesha, Wisconsin, in 2014. It is very different to traditional urban legends in the style of its creation and the speed and extent of its transmission, all of which began with the internet.

Brunvand (1999) discusses the manner in which an incident such as an excruciatingly embarrassing case of mistaken identity can expand from a simple amusing anecdote into an extended version with extra detail, transforming into a legend. Mistaken identity is so commonplace that such a story is portable and thus can be found worldwide. The premise of the story is always the same, but there are endless variations, such as that quoted by Brunvand in which a dinner guest in London, failing to recognise the person sitting next to them, asks her what she does and is told that she is 'still being the Queen of England's sister'.[2] That would certainly be the kind of story one could 'dine out on' for years to come. It also demonstrates the portability of the story because all you need for it to work is an imbalance of power, with the hapless protagonist always coming off worst following a suitably witty riposte from the person with superior status.

I have seen several stories online where a manager is treated rudely by a random passenger on public transport, only to find that person sitting opposite them in the candidate's chair later that day while they are conducting job interviews. That is not in itself a case of mistaken identity, but it does feature the kind of tight storytelling and ironic, offence-appropriate karma that are characteristic of urban legends.

Slenderman is very different. It began life on the website www.something-awful.com in June 2009. Something Awful is a site that houses a variety of humorous content, including blogs, digital imagery and a variety of fora. An invitation was posted on a forum thread asking people to create a credible spooky character. User Victor Surge posted two photoshopped images of children

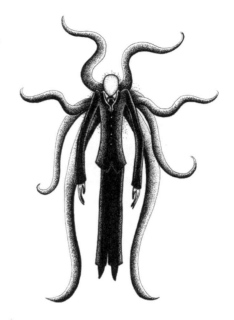

Slenderman. (Illustration by Kathryn Avent)

playing in a park, with a tall, unnaturally thin, faceless figure in the background. The figure is not interacting with the children in any way, just standing there watching. It is wearing a dark suit and seems to have elongated arms and legs, which marks it out as 'other', yet its inclusion in the photos is subtle rather than overt; the viewer's attention is drawn first to the children, as the main focus, and the images need to be studied before the unusual figure is noticed.

The images were accompanied by excellent captions referencing a fire in a library in such a way as to imply that the details of the incident were already common knowledge. The captions also indicated that fourteen children had gone missing that day and noted that the photographer is also believed to be missing. This gave the images both an air of mystery and instant authenticity, as they hinted at a wider back story and the details were scant enough to be suggestive rather than conclusive.

The Slenderman character became incredibly popular on the forum, with users contributing their own 'anecdotes', writing fan fiction, commenting on each other's stories and working together to create a history for the creature. More images appeared, including some purporting to be medieval woodcuts that showed a tall, thin, dark-suited figure and were aimed at establishing a longevity for Slenderman. It is interesting that the woodcuts depict the ubiquitous – and, in this context, anachronistic – black suit for which the character is particularly known.

Over time, the mythos expanded, and it wasn't long before people started sharing sightings and personal experiences of Slenderman, all with a wonderfully genuine ring to them. Drawing on ghost stories, paranormal investigation and centuries of folklore, these 'sightings' also had an air of authenticity about them, as the online community in which they were originally shared had established some parameters for stories about this constructed creature.

One instruction stated that all such anecdotes had to be personal experiences, thus moving them away from the 'friend of a friend' stories we usually expect in urban legends. The community adhered to these guidelines, entering into the spirit of the collaborative process with great enthusiasm, advising each other on how to improve their submissions, and highlighting and discarding any inclusions that did not seem to fit the Slenderman story as it expanded, and thus creating a group identity, rather than reinforcing an existing one, as we find in traditional folklore.

Five years after its creation, Slenderman hit the news when two 12-year-old girls lured a friend into the woods near their homes and stabbed her nineteen times. They claimed they had to do it for Slenderman, as they wanted to become his 'proxies' (servants). Miraculously, the victim survived, and her two attackers are now in secure facilities. Both have since been discovered to have suffered from mental health issues. Despite all the evidence to the contrary, both believed implicitly that Slenderman was real and would attack their families if they did not carry out this horrific act.

The creation of Slenderman has given rise to some interesting inversions when compared with long-standing folkloric legends, such as that of ghostly black dog sightings. Slenderman the character appeared first, and the mythos was created around him with subsequent alleged 'real-life experiences' drawing on aspects of that constructed history and adding to its air of authority, while simultaneously acknowledging that he was not real.

Black dog sightings, on the other hand, are often experienced by people who have no idea at the time that their strange encounter even has a mythos, let alone one that stretches back to the twelfth century and beyond, yet their stories echo countless others. Here, the personal experience gives rise to the story, which then feeds into the folklore.

Yet despite this, belief in Slenderman seems to be comparable to belief in long-established folkloric figures. Is that because his creators drew on aspects of folkloric tradition to give him an aura of familiarity in the midst of his otherness? Is it simply because people understand and acknowledge the link between these modern-day, constructed texts and the folklore on which they are loosely based, while simultaneously believing that there is a slim possibility that Slenderman could exist? Some people do, after all, enjoy being scared, and the aim of the invitation that led to Slenderman's creation in the first place was to create a believable, scary character. Or is belief in Slenderman so strong because he has come to represent something else ... our fears?

We have always used stories to make sense of the world around us, and that is just as true today as it was in the distant past. Slenderman is, at its roots, simply a collection of stories deliberately presented in an authoritative manner designed to encourage belief. In this, we can see echoes of two earlier stories, both of which utilised media and technology to present an 'othered' creature in a similarly authoritative manner, and both of which sparked panic in their audiences. These stories also echoed or highlighted current societal concerns, much as Slenderman did after the Waukesha tragedy.

The first of these stories is H.G. Wells's science fiction novel *War of the Worlds*. Written in 1897, it described an extra-terrestrial invasion of Earth and was serialised as a radio drama by Orson Welles in 1938. It was presented in the style of radio announcements and voiced by Welles himself, adding a further layer of gravitas and authority. At the time, the media released stories claiming that thousands of people had run outside in terror, believing the broadcasts to be real, but it seems likely that such claims were exaggerated. The media's motives for doing this remain unclear, but the Second World War was not far away and they may have chosen to play on people's fear of invasion.

Similarly, the BBC programme *Ghostwatch*, which was aired on Halloween 1992, was presented as a documentary, featuring broadcasting heavyweight Michael Parkinson as one of its main sources of gravitas. Despite listings in TV magazines in which the names of the participating actors were clearly given, the programme caused controversy and has never been aired again.

Taking inspiration from the Enfield Poltergeist case, the programme switched between a live outside broadcast featuring Sarah Greene, leading a camera crew at the scene of an alleged poltergeist haunting, and the TV studio, where Michael Parkinson discussed the case with a psychologist, while fellow presenter Mike Smith oversaw the phone-in. Viewers were invited to share their experiences during the show, but those featured on air were obviously also actors. Although the phone line was live, there was a message telling callers that the show was fiction. The writer, Stephen Volk, was also credited during the opening titles, but those tuning in late would naturally have missed this. As a result, the BBC received harsh criticism and the programme was briefly blamed for causing PTSD (post-traumatic stress disorder) symptoms in children who watched it.

These two examples clearly demonstrate the extent to which belief can be generated in a fictional story. Like Slenderman, both *War of the Worlds* and *Ghostwatch* were clearly fiction, and identified as such, yet when taken out of context, the style of their presentation made the boundary between fact and fiction very unclear, or even removed it altogether. The images of Slenderman, when circulated without context, are no different. A quick search for 'Slenderman' online returns numerous images in all styles – photoshop, hand drawn, digital art – but all remaining faithful to the tall, thin figure in the dark suit that Victor Surge originally posted on the Something Awful website. There are many with repeated motifs such as the woods and the tentacles emerging from his back. In some, he is presented as dynamic, while in others, he simply stands, watching, staring straight through the fourth wall at the viewer.

Slenderman and *Ghostwatch* also share, to a certain degree, the concept of community involvement in the creation of what is, ultimately, a piece of entertainment. Being invited to phone the TV studio with one's own sightings gave BBC viewers a vested interest in the story and undoubtedly held their attention far more successfully than if it had simply been a scary movie. The inclusion of the character 'Pipes', who appears in the background several times throughout the programme, would also have served to both heighten fear and retain the attention of the viewers who spotted him, as well as potentially making them hyper-vigilant in looking out for him thereafter.

The impact of the character's unexpected appearances during the 1992 airing cannot be understated. No one would have been expecting to 'see' a 'ghost'. This is an enhancement that still works today, even after repeated viewings and with the full knowledge of when Pipes is due to make an appearance, it still draws the viewer in just as effectively, especially given the quality of the special effects of the 1990s compared with those of today. In fact, Pipes was entirely practical, a combination of make-up and costume, clever camera work and direction, and with actor Keith Ferrari posing and then ducking off-camera between shots.

This inclusion of the audience in both the Slenderman mythos and the transmission of *Ghostwatch* demonstrates the extent to which the boundary between truth and fiction has been dissolved. The audience or viewer ceases to be fully passive. In the case of *Ghostwatch*, even if, ultimately, they did not see anything that was worthy of a call to the phone-in team, they were actively engaged in looking for something and there was still potential to become personally involved.

Slenderman, of course, relies entirely on people becoming personally involved. This necessarily means that such individuals are placed in the position of having to determine their own version of the truth, rather than having it neatly presented to them as they would if they were passively watching a horror movie or similar.

The issue of belief becomes more complex when Slenderman images or anecdotes are discovered out of context, similar to those people who did not realise that either *War of the Worlds* or *Ghostwatch* were works of fiction. All three are ground-breaking in their own way and the listeners of 1938 and viewers of 1992 could be forgiven for any overreaction to what they heard or saw.

But what of today's tech-savvy audiences, especially those who, like some on the Slenderman forum threads, acknowledge that he is a created construct, yet still confess to being afraid of him? Does this belief help to shift the folkloresque (that which resembles, but is not, folklore) more towards tradition by bringing it into the real world?

Unpacking the issues surrounding the panic following the Waukesha stabbing, it becomes clear that the issue was less about Slenderman himself than what he represented: the safety of children online. Folklorist Dr Andrea Kitta (2018) flags up an interesting point that can often be overlooked today. With generations growing up alongside the internet, the omnipresence of the internet generally and an increasing number of 'silver surfers', it is easy to forget that there are generations who do not use the internet at all and remain deeply suspicious of it, while there are plenty of users who exercise caution regarding both its use and the veracity of the information it offers.

Kitta argues that for those for whom the internet is simply a fact of life, the line between their online worlds and the real world is blurred, or even non-existent.[3] Teenagers communicate online as much as in person, and some, including my 13-year-old daughter, with whom I had an interesting discussion on the subject, do not even differentiate between the two. Much as our ancestors are unlikely to have differentiated between magic and religion, viewing the two as aspects of an overarching belief system, so it is for teens like my daughter, who see both online and in-person communication simply as chatting with friends – the medium is largely unimportant. Of course, as my daughter pointed out, nuances are lost over text chat, and they do not 'mess around' with each other as much when they are online (probably a good thing!) but in spite of those distinctions, she does not consciously think in terms of 'online' or 'real-world' communication, grouping everything together under the umbrella of 'chatting with friends'. There is certainly nothing to distinguish any of the media my daughter uses (both real-life and virtual) from each other. For her, they all have value; contact with her friends is the important thing, not the method by which that interaction occurs.

Regardless of what we, as individuals, think about the internet and its potential dangers, it cannot be denied that it has infiltrated our lives in ways in which we may no longer be consciously aware. Social media is the one area where we can see countless examples of this. How many of us, when sitting in front of a delicious meal in a restaurant, pause to capture a photo before tucking in? How many of us take selfies, or whip out our phones to video something? These are all new aspects of our collective behaviour that have only been introduced to the population at large since the advent of social media such as Facebook, Twitter, Instagram, Tik Tok and Snapchat.

In fact, it has almost become expected behaviour. I have asked, and been asked, on several occasions, 'Did you get a photo/video?' at the end of an anecdote (usually, I didn't).

Yet, while this might be seen as the creeping onslaught of the online world, where everyone is desperately chasing 'likes' and followers, I would argue that it also demonstrates the basic desire of humans to share stories and experiences. Capturing a photo heightens the experience for the other person, being able to share a video with them is even better. In some cases, it helps to preserve the original story, while enabling others to share the experience vicariously at a later date and, perhaps, strengthening bonds between those sharing the photos or video and those consuming.

The post-Waukesha panic regarding online safety echoed the 'Satanic Panic' of the 1970s and 1980s, which arose in respect of a general fear about satanic rituals taking place, and which targeted heavy metal music and the role-playing game *Dungeons and Dragons*, among other things, as 'bad influences' on young children. This kind of mass hysteria has been seen on numerous occasions, such as the media encouraging people to burn their video nasties and thus escalating and blowing situations out of proportion. *War of the Worlds* amplified a fear of invasion, while *Ghostwatch* and Slenderman highlighted concerns about what young children were being exposed to in the mass media.

Kitta also suggests that Slenderman's appearance represents both faceless, exploitative corporations and the universal sensation of being watched, and his creation anthropomorphises and gives a focus to a fear that is otherwise difficult to verbalise.[4] This may, in part, have contributed to Slenderman's popularity, for no matter who or where we are, we have all, at some point, felt an unseen pair of eyes on us and experienced a degree of discomfort or fear as a result. As geographical barriers do not exist online, this fear is able to ripple further afield than would normally be the case with oral transmission of folk tales or urban legends.

Mark Norman (2015) provides an excellent example, in his book *Black Dog Folklore*, of the manner in which geographical restrictions can skew interpretation. He describes a map of sightings of ghostly black dogs in England, which clearly shows three hotspots: one in Devon, one in Somerset and one in Lincolnshire. Out of context, it appears that sightings are concentrated in these three areas and are rather scant elsewhere in the country. However, the three hotspots indicate nothing more nor less than the areas in which three prominent folklorists were operating. Theo Brown lived in Devon, Ruth L. Tongue in Somerset and Ethel Rudkin in Lincolnshire. The folklore they collected is, as a result, naturally clustered around their homes. The gazetteer of sightings appended to *Black Dog Folklore* demonstrates more clearly the actual extent of this piece of folklore in England and is an excellent illustration of how reliance upon this map has undoubtedly provided an inaccurate view of the distribution of ghostly black dog sightings.[5]

Mass hysteria has always been with us. One has only to look back in the historical record to the witch trials of Salem, Massachusetts, for a prime example. Similarly, urban legends have been inspiring panics and hysteria throughout their long history.

The Victorian era saw a significant number of such panics, inflamed by the actions and responses of the mass media of the day. Foreshadowing the 1980s panic about baby alligators being taken home as pets and subsequently flushed down the toilet into the sewer system of New York, 1859 London was overtaken by a panic about the Sewer Pigs of Hampstead.

The sewer pigs were thought to be a monstrous porcine family living entirely below ground in the London sewer system, and even featured in the *Daily Telegraph* newspaper. A sow had apparently become trapped, it was said, and had given birth to a litter of piglets, the entire family living off the rubbish that accumulated in the sewers and producing litter after litter. The population lived in fear of these terrible creatures escaping from the sewer system and running riot throughout London.

Obviously, there is nothing within a sewer system that would sustain a pig, let alone a number of them. The fear connected to this particular urban legend is disease and it arose after the hot summer of 1858 caused a devastating outbreak of typhoid and cholera in the city. Unsurprisingly, there has never been any evidence of pigs in London's sewers, monstrous, lost or otherwise.

The pig panic was followed a few years later by the Garrotting Panic of 1862, again in London. This centred on 'garrotting gangs' comprising a 'back-stall' or lookout (a role often undertaken by a woman), a 'front-stall', who apprehended the victim, and the 'nasty-man', who wielded the garrotte. Such gangs would ambush unsuspecting victims, attacking and robbing them. These gangs had been a reality on London's streets since Tudor times, but there was media focus on them after a couple of high-profile cases. One of these was Edward Hawkins, an antiquary in his eighties, and the other was a Member of Parliament, Hugh Pilkington, who was attacked in broad daylight as he left the House of Commons, losing his watch to the thieves and receiving a head injury.

The fear stirred up and amplified by the media on this occasion involves changes to the criminal justice system. Prisoners were no longer being transported to the colonies; instead they were being released back into their communities after serving their sentences, constituting a new type of threat. Previously, people had never really had to think about convicted prisoners, as once they set out for their new destination, it was unlikely that they would ever return. Therefore, recidivism was not particularly important in England as, if it was going to happen, it was on someone else's doorstep.

When transportation stopped, recidivism and the threat from convicted criminals suddenly became a stark reality in England and the Pilkington attack was one of the crimes the media used to spotlight the issue. Naturally, this did very little to assist the efforts of those campaigning for prison reforms, especially as the newspapers featured articles comparing the streets of London to well-known, dangerous areas abroad, which heightened people's fears.

The police were criticised for their perceived ineffectiveness and the combination of poor policing and media focus on what was deemed a very 'un-British' crime fanned the flames of the panic. People hired guards to escort them around the city and bought anti-garrotting devices that were created in response to the panic. In 1856, *Punch* magazine published a humorous cartoon showing a gentleman in a top hat, wearing an overcoat that had been fitted with a crinoline.[6] Behind him, a garrotter reaches out to him, scarf in hand, but is stopped by the radius of the crinoline, which is too great to allow him to reach his intended victim. The issue was still ongoing in 1892, when more press reports were circulated about garrotting gangs in London.

However, while it is easy to lump all newspapers together under the banner of 'the media', not all of them took part in the manufacture of this panic. Several dismissed it entirely, stating that the stories were being blown out of proportion. Yes, there were occasionally attacks of this nature in London, but sensationalism took over and instilled in the general public a belief that there were former convicts on every street corner, waiting for their next victim. Once the media had captured the imagination of the public, the protestations of these more reasonable publications were lost.

Prior to the threat of attack by terrifying subterranean pigs, London had experienced a very different kind of threat. Spring-Heeled Jack was first reported in London in 1837 after a young girl named Mary Stevens was attacked on Clapham Common one evening as she made her way home after visiting her parents. A figure leapt out at her from an alley, grabbed her in his arms and began kissing her and tearing at her clothes. Mary later stated that her attacker's hands were as cold as a corpse's and that he seemed to have claws. Her screams sent the man fleeing into the darkness and roused people living nearby, who came to her assistance and searched for her attacker, but he had vanished.

The following night, not far from Mary Stevens's home, a man leapt out in front of a carriage, causing the driver to lose control and crash. The driver was badly injured in the accident. The perpetrator again escaped. This time, witnesses stated that he leaped over a wall around 9ft high, laughing maniacally. It was feats such as this that earned him his name.

A few months later, at the beginning of 1838, the Lord Mayor of London revealed a number of letters that had been received by his office from various parts of the city, all complaining about pranks being played on people by someone disguised variously as a ghost or a devil. The complaints described victims so frightened by these attacks that some had suffered fits as a result, while others had been wounded by claw-like appendages the attacker used as part of his costume. Some, it was claimed, had even died after being attacked.

By April that year, the press were referring to the attacker as Spring-Heeled Jack. The character grew in notoriety, with several other high-profile attacks reported in the newspapers. After this, reports dwindled until around 1843, when a fresh set of incidents occurred. This time, however, they were not focused in London.

There were attacks of various kinds in places as far afield as Devon, East Anglia and Northampton. Some involved coach drivers, others were assaults. The attacker was described as being horned like the Devil, with flaming red eyes.

Jack was, by this time, a popular figure in penny dreadfuls, which would, undoubtedly, have carried information about his activities well beyond the distribution area of the London newspapers. In 1872, the 'Peckham Ghost' appeared in the press in an article in the *News of the World*, which claimed it was Spring-Heeled Jack up to his old tricks again. There were sporadic sightings thereafter, including one from Aldershot Barracks in the late 1870s. A group of soldiers were accosted by a strange figure who slapped one man

144   THE BOY'S STANDARD.

Published Weekly.   NOW READY.   Price One Penny.

NOS. 1 AND 2 (TWENTY-FOUR PAGES), SPLENDIDLY ILLUSTRATED, IN HANDSOME WRAPPER.

The History of this Remarkable Being has been specially compiled, for this work only, by one of the Best Authors of the day, and our readers will find that he has undoubtedly succeeded in producing a Wonderful and Sensational Story, every page of which is replete with details of absorbing and thrilling interest.

Advertisement for Spring-Heeled Jack penny dreadful, 1886.

around the face before escaping unscathed by the bullets that were then shot at him. He was described by the soldiers as moving in great bounding leaps.

129

What exactly was the motivation behind Spring-Heeled Jack? No one was ever held accountable for his crimes and, given the geographical spread and the decades that passed between his first and final appearances, it is safe to say that there were several people behind the crimes attributed to him.

Spring-Heeled Jack is a form of ghost hoaxing, a type of ostensive prank where perpetrators dress up in often elaborate, spooky costumes for the express purpose of scaring others. This phenomenon was also seen in Australia, as Dr David Waldron explains in an episode of 'The Folklore Podcast'.[7]

> Australian ghost hoaxers also wore elaborate costumes and frequently employed phosphorus as a means of adding an ethereal, ghostly glow. Some hoaxers committed serious assaults, others, such as British elocutionist Herbert Patrick MacLennan, worked a respectable job by day and ran around the streets by night exposing his genitals to women. There was also a case where a woman dressed as a man and, having engaged in conversation with people and convinced them that she was male, would then expose herself and reveal that she was female. She was charged with indecent exposure and ended up in an asylum. On release, she would dress in a glow-in-the-dark robe and hideous mask and hide under bridges in order to leap out at passers-by.

What we see here is a variety of people using ghost hoaxing as a means to escape conventional societal norms. The respectable clerk becomes a flasher; a woman enjoys the freedom of pretending to be a man. Obviously, some hoaxers clearly used their disguises as a means to commit serious crimes, but for others, it seems to have been a way to explore aspects of their personality that societal boundaries rendered an impossibility. The elaborate costumes and the time it must have taken to craft them suggests that most, if not all of the people involved in ghost hoaxing must have had a fairly decent income and the luxury of free time in which to put their outfits together, and that they were perhaps middle class and fairly well educated.

This kind of ostensive practice reflected popular culture; in the Victorian era, this would have been the characters or subjects found in plays or in penny dreadfuls, such as Spring-Heeled Jack. Again, this supports the theory that these were educated people with disposable income to spend on reading materials and theatre tickets as well as costume components.

Today, we find people cosplaying as characters such as Slenderman or creepy clowns and undertaking legend tripping, which, as discussed in Chapter 5, involves visiting the location of a legend or crime and either re-enacting it or trying to experience it through interaction and immersion in the atmosphere of the place. This can involve elaborate, detailed costumes or props, depending on how invested the participants are in the story.

We looked at the folklore of Cabell's tomb in Chapter 2, which is a form of simple legend tripping for which no costumes, props or equipment is required; one is supposed to walk around the tomb and then put a finger through the bars or keyhole for the Devil or Cabell to nibble. There is an excellent example of legend tripping in the 2011 TV series *American Horror Story*. In Season 1, Episode 2, the Harmon family, who have moved into a house in which numerous murders have occurred, are victims of a home invasion by three legend trippers on the anniversary of a 1968 double murder. They are all serial killer devotees and intend to re-enact the crime, forcing Vivien Harmon and her daughter Violet to play the roles of the two victims. All three of the legend trippers are deeply invested, providing era-accurate outfits for their two victims, as well as bringing weapons and other props to enhance the authenticity of their experience.

Victorian ghost hoaxing was a very personal issue, with perpetrators only able to interact with their victims on a one-to-one basis for the most part. Whereas Slenderman fans can converse with any number of like-minded people online, and thus share their experiences or the fear they wish to transmit to a potentially global audience, legend tripping is more individual and personal, and not intended for an audience other than those directly involved in the re-enactment, thus harking back to the experiences of the unfortunate victims of characters such as Spring-Heeled Jack.

It is interesting to note that as time went on, Spring-Heeled Jack's appearance in fiction shifted significantly from the role of villain to that of superhero. A character known as Pérák, the Spring Man, who shared a number of Jack's characteristics, featured in Czechoslovakian science fiction and comics, usually as a hero and often in response to Nazi and Russian propaganda. He first appeared in comic form in 1948, and as recently as 2008, featured in a satirical comic strip by Czech writer Ondřej Neff, in which he was opposed by a villain called Globalman.

Pérák's otherworldly characteristics, including impossibly high jumps, fed into his superhero status, whereas they had been used, along with glowing red eyes and breathing blue fire, to classify Jack as something alien or demonic. We see something similar in Slenderman fan fiction, where the character is sometimes used not as a threat to the writer, but rather as a kind of avenging angel working on their behalf. This enables writers to exorcise their inner demons, perhaps as a result of bullying, turning the full wrath of Slenderman on those who have hurt them.

Both characters have also attained 'bogeyman' status, although, as you might expect in Victorian times, Spring-Heeled Jack was used as a cautionary tale by parents. Slenderman, despite having escaped the confines of his virtual world, has never really been an intergenerational figure of fear in the same way. Rather, he is used to transmit fear between peers, either for a shared experience or something rather more sinister and unpleasant.

Two recent urban legends where a similar peer-to-peer transmission of fear is demonstrated are the Blue Whale Challenge and the Momo Challenge. Like the Satanic Panic, which arose out of misplaced fears about evil adults, believed to be Satanists, preying on vulnerable children, Blue Whale also had its share of rumours about child abuse, albeit in an online context.

The Satanic Panic began in the USA and slowly migrated across the country and overseas into Britain and parts of Europe. Blue Whale originated in Russia in around 2016, first being mentioned in the press in connection with over 100 deaths in the country that were linked to some type of online coercion. Investigators attempted to infiltrate internet groups to determine what was happening, as there were reports of young people being instructed to cut words into their skin and undertake other unpleasant and potentially dangerous activities, fifty in total, which escalated over a period of time from initially harmless acts, such as drawing a picture of a whale, and culminated in the final challenge – taking one's own life.

The general hysteria about predatory adults targeting vulnerable young people online was further fuelled when one of the admins of an online Blue Whale group admitted that he had encouraged fifteen teenagers to take their own lives. Yet it seems that this man was the exception rather than the rule, and the alleged links between Blue Whale and several cases of suicide became inflated and exaggerated as a result. Investigators discovered that the admins of the Blue Whale groups were, in fact, young people – teenagers, rather than adults – carrying out what is essentially a mass campaign of cyberbullying.

Unlike ghost hoaxing, where there are either individual victims or perhaps small groups on occasion, use of online forum threads enables a single person to reach and influence countless others across the globe, and the kind of dares found within the challenge are consistent with what we might expect to see in the more traditional form of bullying. As we have seen with Slenderman, young people caught up in Blue Whale believed that the admins would harm them or their families if they failed to complete any part of the challenge. There was also a significant fear about devices being hacked by admins so they could learn all about the victims' families and thus be able to target and attack them more efficiently and effectively.[8]

This once again raised issues seen in the aftermath of Waukesha in relation to Slenderman – online safety and the targeting of young people within the digital world. Today, young people cannot simply physically remove themselves to escape their bullies. Geographical barriers are swept away, as phones and computers enable bullies to be with their victims anywhere and at any time. This raises the question of safe spaces for young people and fuels the argument of those who believe the internet is dangerous. Yet despite Blue Whale's victims being available twenty-four hours a day, and although it has been mentioned in several suicide cases from countries worldwide, it has not been definitely linked to any of them.

The most recent of this type of challenge is the 2018 Momo Challenge, which, again, originated online in the form of a series of tasks to be completed, with threats being made by a character called 'Momo' if a victim refused. After being in the news for a few months, the hubbub died, only to resurface in 2019 with reports of clips featuring Momo being inserted into innocuous children's videos on YouTube, such as *Peppa Pig*. In addition, images of a bizarre-looking creature with a humanoid head, huge bulging eyes, long, straggling dark hair, an unnaturally wide, beak-like mouth, a tiny body and large birdlike feet began to appear online. This creature was, it was alleged, Momo, and it would send threatening private messages via WhatsApp to those participating in the challenge to ensure compliance. Often, it was reported, these messages contained offensive, graphic or gory images, and it was this kind of image that was apparently inserted into the children's videos.

Schools in the UK picked up on this story and took action to warn parents, although there do not seem to have been any reports of actual incidents. Our daughter's school sent letters detailing the kinds of activity parents needed to look out for on their children's devices. I investigated the issue and what I saw online echoed what was in the letter, but on consulting Snopes.com, an excellent urban legend fact-checking website, it appeared that the phenomenon was unproven. Nonetheless, we raised the subject with our daughter in one of our conversations about her internet usage. She recalls at least one person speaking about Momo in school, but her internet usage was relatively limited so she had seen very little online herself. It was the image of what she terms 'the creepy chicken-woman thing' that remained with her, and when I spoke to her about it recently, she was unable to recall having seen anything beyond that.

Investigation revealed a surprising lack of evidence for such a widespread phenomenon, especially given that those undertaking the challenge were required to provide photographic or video evidence of their compliance. In the UK, a concerned mother appeared on news sites in February 2019 with a warning about the Momo Challenge. Her young son had been told by classmates to watch a video about it and threats were made that if he did not, Momo would come after him. The boy did not engage in the challenge, nor was there any direct contact with Momo, but he did watch the video, which upset him.

This report seems to have been the catalyst for the action taken by schools, but, as with most urban legends, the story's actual origins cannot be pinpointed. Ultimately, the Momo creature was revealed to have been a sculpture by Japanese special effects company Link Factory. It had been in an exhibition in 2016 and images of it were appropriated and attached to the Momo Challenge. The company itself denied any involvement, and the sculpture, which was crafted from perishable materials, was thrown away in 2018 when it started to decompose.

The Momo panic has been reported worldwide in countries such as Argentina, Canada, Pakistan, Ireland and Brunei, as well as the

USA and the UK. There were countless rumours about links to suicides – all unproven – but authorities in Pakistan were sufficiently concerned that a law was passed to make distribution of both Momo and Blue Whale illegal.

Slenderman and Momo have both given rise to movies or first-person survival video games in which the player must avoid the character and survive until the main objective is achieved. In one of the Slenderman games, this involves collecting eight items that have been hidden in a forest. The objective in the Momo game is to complete a series of tasks and remain alive until the police arrive to rescue you from the house in which you have been trapped.

In providing a new medium through which users can interact with the mythos of Slenderman and, to a far lesser extent, that of Momo, these characters bridge the divide between the folkloresque and folklore, depending on the context and who is engaging with them. For example, we are probably more likely to hear about them via word of mouth, just as our ancestors learned their legends. Can they be classified as one or the other now, or has this shift in transmission finally lifted these characters and others like them out of the folkloresque and made them folklore?

Let us consider the Cottingley fairies for a moment. This well-known hoax from 1917, created by Frances Griffiths, aged 9, and her cousin Elsie Wright, aged 16, consisted of five photographs featuring one or other of the girls interacting with what appeared to be fairies. These images succeeded in fooling many people, not least Sir Arthur Conan Doyle, who became deeply involved and believed it publicly and wholeheartedly. To him, the apparent existence of fairies validated his spiritualist beliefs by proving that there was clearly otherworldly activity occurring.

Doyle was writing an article on fairies for the *Strand* magazine when the photos first appeared, and he ended up working alongside Edward Gardner of the Bradford Theosophical Society to have them authenticated. The results of these efforts, like public reactions in the press, were mixed. Some people, including Elsie Wright's photographer father, dismissed the photos as an obvious hoax, while others, including Elsie's mother Polly, believed them to be genuine. Doyle was given permission to use the images alongside his article.

The phenomenon took hold and soon snowballed far beyond what either of the girls had expected when they took the photos. It was not until 1921 that interest began to wane, by which time the girls were fed up with the whole situation and enjoyed playing along with the various experts who visited them to catch their own glimpse of the fairies and undertake investigations. In 1983, an article appeared in *The Unexplained* magazine, in which the cousins admitted that the photos had been faked using cut-outs from a popular fairy book, and thus vindicating the numerous detractors who had pointed sceptically to, among other things, the surprisingly fashionable hairstyles the fairies were sporting.[9]

Paul Manning (2018) discusses the similarity between the Slenderman and Cottingley photos.[10] Both can be traced to their precise origin, and both were removed from their original forum and thus from their original context. The fact that both began with photos adds to their out-of-context authenticity; this was particularly relevant to the Cottingley images. Whereas photographic manipulation and enhancement is the norm today, it was not necessarily the first thing that would have occurred to people at the beginning of the twentieth century when, as the old saying goes, 'the camera never lies'. Of course, several experts who examined the Cottingley images at the time clearly stated that the camera had lied in this instance.

Manning suggests that Conan Doyle appropriated the Cottingley images for his own purposes, and although he did seek permission from Elsie Wright's father Arthur to have them printed in the *Strand* alongside his article, it is unlikely that Wright, who firmly believed the photos were a prank, would have given permission for them to be subjected to the tests and opinions of the various experts whom Conan Doyle consulted. Once removed from their original, intended context, the images enabled viewers to attach their own beliefs and opinions, in much the same way as members of the Slenderman community do with the various constructions around 'their' creature.

The main difference with these two sets of images is that one was known from the outset to be a construct, whereas Cottingley was only suspected to be such, and not by everyone. Both sets of images involved a degree of manipulation and both were originally intended for entertainment purposes only, yet such is the need in humans to believe in that which we cannot see, both Cottingley and Slenderman were transformed by people other than their original creators into something more. The aspects of folklore on which those creators drew has served to secure their places in people's minds as representations of the possibility of the otherworldly.

Interestingly, another virtual space in which something akin to an urban legend has arisen is that of Second Life, an immersive, online 3D world launched in 2003, in which users can create an avatar to interact with a seemingly endless variety of items, experiences, virtual locations and other peoples' avatars. Its status as either a game, a virtual world or a social media platform has long been debated, and users tend to have strong, individual views on the subject. Second Life has its own currency, a unit called 'lindens', and it is around this that the putative urban legend has arisen.

Essentially, an avatar called 'Kevin', or a variation thereof, usually with numbers suffixed, randomly messages another avatar, explaining that he is new to Second Life and has raised a small amount of 'lindens', but needs a little more to buy something to improve his avatar's appearance, or to pay rent of some kind. He asks the avatar if they would be prepared to give him the rest of the 'lindens' he needs.

A Second Life user showed me some of the comments regarding 'Kevin' that appeared early in 2021 in a Facebook group they belong to. The 'Kevin' character is clearly notorious for this behaviour, asking for amounts ranging from 250 to 750 'lindens' for a variety of reasons. (For context, 2,000 'lindens' costs roughly US$20 – so in real-world terms, we are talking about pocket change here.)

As well as describing these messages as a scam, users in the Facebook group also react to them with amusement, as this appears to have been ongoing for many years, suggesting that 'Kevin' is not quite as 'new' as he claims to be. In addition, poor 'Kevin' always seems to have precisely the same amount of 'lindens'. Some people gleefully state, 'I've been Kevined!', while others jokingly comment that their life is now complete, as they have received a begging message from 'Kevin'. Some users claim to have been targeted on multiple occasions.

It is unclear whether 'Kevin' is one person or many; it may be that the original has since been joined by copycats, it may be that the original creates a new account each time he is banned from the platform, or it may be some kind of bot. Looking at some of the comments on the posts I was shown, it seems that 'Kevin' favours shopping events, presumably due to their high traffic, which would enable him to efficiently target many users in a short space of time. However, regardless of who or what is behind them, the messages appear to be copy-and-paste, and although some users claim to have received personalised answers when they respond, others state that they had no response, even one user who reportedly offered him 1,000 'lindens'. The majority seem to have either blocked and reported the account, or pointedly told 'Kevin' where to go.

Overall, most users reacted to the original Facebook post with humour, sharing anecdotes of their own experiences, posting amusing fictional anecdotes and commenting on the longevity of this particular scam. This in itself is somewhat of a joke, as some users first encountered 'Kevin' around a decade ago, yet his message invariably says that he is new. 'Kevin' and his numerous iterations are clearly viewed as a mildly irritating joke, although the person who showed me the posts had never heard of him being mentioned among their friends in Second Life itself and did not know any of the users in the Facebook group. Are we in 'a friend of a friend' territory here?

Not quite. The community responses to these Facebook posts were, in nature, reminiscent of comments on the Creepypasta and Something Awful sites, indicating a high level of engagement, an overall familiarity with the subject matter and the sharing of anecdotes (both real and fictional) to add to the story. Yet, is there really any similarity between 'Kevin' and Slenderman? Both, it could be argued, are fictional constructs created online and enhanced with anecdotes and other input from a community. The backgrounds of both are scant on detail. Both have the potential to trigger real, lived experiences, 'Kevin' by scamming people out of virtual currency that has been paid for in US dollars.

I have already mentioned the real-world tragedy attributed to belief in Slenderman and, of course, he also provides endless opportunities to feel genuine fear in the real world. The difference is that behind 'Kevin' there is at least one human being undertaking actions to which others can directly respond and with which they can interact. Although there is a degree of proactivity in the case of 'Kevin', where humorous fictional anecdotes are shared, people are necessarily reactive, responding to 'Kevin' himself.

The Slenderman community is, by contrast, proactive, each member providing their own building block that may or may not find a permanent home within the Slenderman mythos. 'Kevin' is neatly contained within the virtual world of Second Life, whereas Slenderman roams the real world, and all 'Kevin' has with which to challenge Slenderman's mythos is a rather dodgy reputation as a scammer. Can 'Kevin' attain in his virtual world a similar status to that enjoyed by Slenderman in the real world? Only time will tell.

With Slenderman in particular, we have been privileged to see a legend being created, and to gain some insight into how our ancestors' stories attained legendary status over time. Humans love to tell stories, be they dinner party anecdotes, the convoluted tales of the local raconteur in the pub, collaborative efforts, such as we see in role-playing games, or a family passing on favourite stories through the generations. Each style has its own community behaviours, be it simply a knowing, amused nod at the raconteur's exaggerations or maintaining an agreed set of guidelines such as we see in the creation of Slenderman. Although in some cases, as we have seen, personal interaction with stories can result in tragedy, for the most part, we simply become guardians of these stories, preserving them and passing them on to future generations and enjoying them along the way.

REFERENCES

1 Brunvand, J.H., *Too Good to be True – The Colossal Book of Urban Legends* (London and New York: WW Norton & Company Limited, 1999).
2 *Ibid.*
3 Kitta, A., 'What Happens When the Pictures are no Longer Photoshops? – Slenderman, Belief and the Unacknowledged Common Experience' in Blank, T.J. and L.S. McNeill (eds), *Slenderman is Coming – Creepypasta and Contemporary Legends on the Internet* (Louisville: University Press of Colorado, 2018).
4 *Ibid.*
5 Norman, M., *Black Dog Folklore* (London: Troy Books Publishing, 2015).
6 *Punch*, December 1856 (London: Punch Publications Limited).
7 Waldron, D., 'Playing the Ghost' via 'The Folklore Podcast', Series 1, Episode 5, 19 September 2016.
8 Tucker, E. (2020), 'The Blue Whale Suicide Challenge – Hypermodern Ostension on a Global Scale' in Peck, A. and T.J. Blank (eds), *Folklore and Social Media* (Louisville: University Press of Colorado, 2020).
9 Cooper, J., 'Cottingley: At Last, the Truth', *The Unexplained* (117): 2 (1982).
10 Manning, P., 'Monstrous Media and Media Monsters – From Cottingley to Waukesha' in Blank, T.J. & L.S. McNeill (eds), *Slenderman is Coming – Creepypasta and Contemporary Legends on the Internet* (Louisville: University Press of Colorado, 2018).

La Calavera Catrina. (Photo credit: Gzzz, CC BY-SA 4.0)

5

DARK TOURISM AND LEGEND TRIPPING

We all need a break now and again from the rigours of daily life. For some, this might be sitting on a sandy beach somewhere hot, watching groups of people on comically large inflatable bananas being towed along the waterline. For others, it might be careening down a snow-covered mountainside, aiming for terminal velocity while not aiming for the groups of others doing the same. But for a smaller and braver (or possibly foolhardier) few, it could be a bus trip through Chernobyl, lunch on the Cambodian Killing Fields, or buying pens made from spent bullets in a Sarajevo market.

These people are known as the 'Dark Tourists' – individuals who favour a holiday engaging with sites of death, trauma or tragedy. At first glance, it sounds like something that one would not even consider doing for fun. But scratch the surface and you find that there is so much to link this practice to us as human beings, to our past and to our emotional and social connections. A lot of it engages with our cultural heritage and folklore on many levels.

Although increasing in popularity since the 1990s, the concept of dark tourism is far from new. In 1815, members of the European nobility and aristocracy were paying good prices for seats from which to observe the Battle of Waterloo. In the 1860s, picnics were organised in Virginia to allow groups to sit and snack, while watching the first large battle of the American Civil War. Two days later, some of these spectators bought the battlefield to market to visitors as a tourist attraction.

Humans have always been fascinated by death. On a psychological level, this should be no great surprise as it ultimately affects us all. From ancient times we have records of many cults who worshipped death gods such as Anubis (the guardian of poisons) and Osiris (the king of the dead). Some of these figures are no longer revered in the same way, but others are still playing a very important part in some cultures, such as the figure of Santa Muerte, whose cult we will examine later in this chapter.

The term 'dark tourism' was first used in 1996 by Malcolm Foley and John J. Lennon in an article for the *International Journal of Heritage Studies* on the fascination that people had with the assassination of President Kennedy.[1] They defined it as 'the presentation and consumption (by visitors) of real and commodified death and disaster sites'.

A later term came into play to narrow down this field to those activities that specifically involved the interplay with death itself. This was 'Thana tourism', taking as its root the Greek word for death, *Thanatos*. This subset of dark tourism concentrates on activities 'associated with death, anguish, pain, carnage, warfare, calamities and disasters – the unspoken essence of human existence'.[2]

Writing for the journal *Tourism* in 2006, Philip Stone notes that 'death has been an element of tourism longer than any other form of tourism supply'.[3] The Colosseum in Rome might be viewed in this way, as one of the first attractions catering to dark tourism. In many ways, this form of tourism may be seen as a part of heritage tourism – learning through interaction with our past.

Thana tourism involves the tourist making a connection between themselves and the deceased, engaging with the social integration of the death.[4] This concept became evident very quickly after people began visiting the spot where Princess Diana's car crashed in Paris. Subsequently, the railings and lawns at Kensington Palace turned into a shrine to the late princess, with flowers, messages and tokens being left in one of the world's largest contemporary assemblages on an unprecedented scale. Mourners travelled from all over the world to both visit the shrine and make their own offerings. This has since been viewed as an example of mass hysteria not unlike the alleged reaction to Orson Welles's production of *War of the Worlds* (see Chapter 4).

Many people undertake a simple form of dark tourism without even realising it, such as when visiting the iconic Taj Mahal in India. For all its beauty and splendour as a piece of architecture and recognisability as a prime spot for holiday photographs, it is, at the end of the day, a mausoleum containing (at least) the bodies of the Mughal Emperor Shah Jahān and his wife, Mumtaz Mahal, in whose memory the emperor constructed the building.

There is a myth, probably as unknown to many of the tourists visiting as the fact that they are partaking in dark tourism by even being there, that there is a third grave somewhere in the Taj Mahal. Some scholars believe that evidence for this stems from the fact that there is a Turkish Mughal tradition, found in other prominent tombs of the period, for there to be three sets of graves in a mausoleum.[5] This idea is, however, only a theory as nothing has yet been found to prove that a third set exists in this case. It is likely that the 'graves' of the emperor and his wife are not the actual ones that are able to be visited. Muslim tradition tends to place graves underground so that the bodies are not disturbed until *Yawm ad-Din*, the Day of Judgement, for members of that faith. Likenesses of the graves would be built for public grief or visitation.

While most of the visitors to a location such as the Taj Mahal might not cite the graves as their primary reason for going, the more aware dark tourists would certainly include them among their driving forces. In an article for the journal *Tourism Geographies* on holidays related to war in Korea, Bigley et al. provided a table of motivation factors that drove people to undertake dark tourism. It is worth noting that many of these factors overlap strongly with folklore. From their original table we might pull out the following:

Heritage: A personal connection or identification with site or event.

History: Keen interest in history of site or event; experiential learning

Nostalgia: To experience a 'wistful mood that (results from) a preference or fantasy for something from the past'.

Artefacts: To view material culture, or 'symbolic representations' of such, associated with sites or events – in situ or at alternate locations.

Site sacralization: The process of assigning cultural identity, meaning or value to a site which 'creates' an attraction that can fulfil other motivations (remembrance, education, et al.)[6]

The last of these, site sacralisation, might be seen as especially important in terms of folklore, which is all about ascribing meaning. Sometimes, the meaning might come from a number of interpretations. Consider the site of the Battle of Panipat, which engages with mythology, legend and folklore, as well as being more obviously a site for remembrance.

Panipat, a city that mythology tells us was founded by one of the two family branches featured in the ancient Indian epic *Mahabharata*, has seen three great battles – two in the sixteenth century and one in the eighteenth. Local beliefs say that the red soil found on the battlefield is that colour due to the amount of blood spilled there during the battles. This is a claim that may be ascribed to many battlefield sites and is due to high levels of iron oxide in the ground rather than any bloodshed, which would have been washed away long ago.

Where this idea is taken one stage further still is at the site of the third battle, Kala Amb Park. *Kala Amb* translates as 'Black Mango' and the name comes from a mango tree that used to grow on the site and was purported to have leaves that were darker than those on a normal mango tree. Again, this was said to be due to the tree roots drawing up blood from the soldiers, which also turned the fruits black. It is an interesting local extension on a common battlefield story.

Folklore from this area also tells of the sounds of swords striking each other and screams and cries of agony that can be heard in the Panipat area after midnight. It is clear to see from this example that a visitor to Panipat might engage with the site and its folklore in several ways in order to create meaningful cultural identity and hence fulfil the site sacralisation motivation from the table above.

For many, the interaction with tragedy in dark tourism, or death more specifically in Thana tourism, may be classed as a religious experience. Eric Venbrux, in an article on cemeteries being used in this way, notes that these sorts of visitors may be seen as being on a sacred journey.[7] Trips might be seen in a similar way to more mainstream religious pilgrimages such as to Lourdes, for example. The religiosity of dark tourism might be seen on one level in terms of legend tripping, which we will explore in the second half of this chapter and is a more experiential aspect, but also in terms of more direct interaction with religious events and festivals.

One extremely well-known festival that is a celebration of death is the *Dia de los Muertos*, or Day of the Dead. Found originally, in terms of cultural significance, in Mexico, the recognisable public processional performances and sugar skull offerings are rapidly spreading into other countries through recreations and cultural appropriation that many anthropologists and historians find troubling. Here we focus on the original locating of the festivities in Mexico.

The origins of *Dia de los Muertos* may be traced back over thousands of years to peoples such as the Aztecs, for whom death was not an event to be mourned but rather to be celebrated. Those who had passed away were remembered all year round but were believed to return to earth during the Day of the Dead. As with many religious or quasi-religious celebrations, we find elements of the original rituals combined with those of more Christianised aspects, or other modern religious beliefs. *Dia de los Muertos* is often considered to be intrinsically linked to Halloween. This is a rather simplistic analogy, but it does take place on dates that are also connected with Halloween, 1 and 2 November – All Saints' and All Souls' Days respectively. These are significant dates for the Catholic faith, but also have just as much significance when viewed in terms of the time of harvest. This is the time when the last of the living crops have been brought in and it marks the start of the transition to the dead winter months.

The Day of the Dead has risen to such prominence that in 2008 it was added to the UNESCO register for Intangible Cultural Heritage. Probably the most recognisable symbol associated with the Day of the Dead is the elegant skull figure, Catrina, seen often on the painted faces of women participating in the festival. The origins of this symbol come from an early twentieth-century political cartoon drawn as a personification of death and intended to poke fun at the tendency found in Mexico at the time to copy personal styles from Europe, which were considered to be more sophisticated. The meaning behind this was to suggest that despite the infinite variety of ways in which Mexicans chose to present

Santa Muerte. (Illustration by Kathryn Avent)

themselves, and the effort they went to mimicking other cultures, they were all essentially the same underneath. Later, the figure was included in a mural painted by artist Diego Rivera called 'Dream of a Sunday Afternoon in Alameda Park' (1947). Rivera named his version of the original skull Catrina, which was a slang term in Mexico for 'the rich'. This is the version that has been adopted by women today.

Anthropologist Kate Kingsbury notes that death in Mexico is very much seen as a feminine domain.[8] Women are frequently marginalised in Mexico, being tied to the home. However, because funerary rites so often take place at home, this means that the men do not get involved in arrangements or rituals connected with death, creating a rare arena in which females can take a lead. This is seen in the dominance of female figures symbolically connected with death such as Catrina, but also in terms of legend through *La Llorona* (the weeping woman of urban folklore in Mexico) and through religious festivals such as the Cult of Santa Muerte.

Santa Muerte, or Holy Death, is a female saint portrayed in skeletal form and usually clothed in robes not unlike those worn by the Christian figure of Mary. She is one of a number of saints worshipped in Mexico under the banner of what might be termed folk Catholicism – that is, beliefs that are essentially labelled as Catholic, but are modified by indigenous cultures and local behaviours.

The Mexican cults of folk saints are tied in very closely with folk healing practices. Many of the 'saints' are not, in fact, canonised but are figures from whom healing and other magical favours are sought. For a Christian, rather than secular parallel from our own history, we might look to the cult of St Thomas Becket, which was hugely popular in medieval times (see Chapter 3).

The first recorded case of Santa Muerte being worshipped appears to come from a report on idolatry published in 1797. The massive spread of the saint in modern times can be attributed to a couple of women, most notably Doña Queta, who placed the first shrine in the neighbourhood of Tepito in Mexico City.

Doña Queta originally had a small altar in her kitchen, where she had a cottage business selling quesadillas to the local residents.

Tepito is a notoriously dangerous area and the altar had first been set up so that Doña Queta could pray for the safety of her son, who was in jail at the time. Visitors saw the figure of Santa Muerte there and asked if they could leave offerings on the altar. When the prayers being offered up appeared to work and her son was safely released, Doña Queta moved her shrine into the street as a mark of gratitude to the saint and invested the monetary offerings that had been left previously into enlarging the altar. Over time, the street shrine became a site of pilgrimage, and the cult grew rapidly in its public popularity.

This popularity was obviously of great concern to the established Church in the area. Figures of death have been found in Catholic iconography since the thirteenth century. We might think, by way of example, of the proliferation of memento mori reminding viewers of their mortality. The spread of the plague caused death to be at the forefront of everyone's thoughts and hence the personification of death appeared more frequently in art at this time. Now, to avoid losing followers, the Catholic Church demonised devotion to death and bishops began to threaten Catholics with excommunication if they were found to be falsely venerating Santa Muerte. In this first step towards the misrepresentation that the Cult of Santa Muerte is often seen under now, the Argentinian pope at the time branded the saint a symbol of narco-culture – that is, a false idol predominantly worshipped by drug barons and members of that part of the criminal underworld.

This misrepresented image of Santa Muerte as a criminal's saint was taken up by the media, who would have frequently been reporting on these common drug-related issues from the Mexican underworld. Subsequently, she entered popular culture with this image. In the TV series *Breaking Bad*, drug traffickers are seen worshipping at a shrine containing a skeleton wearing a bridal gown. From this status, the saint became adopted as a figure for marginalised people – not only criminals but also sex workers and the

LGBTQ+ community, for example. This is a misconception that is slowly being corrected now, in part due to the rise in dark tourism.

Many visitors now attend street parties and festivals associated with Santa Muerte. In Tepito, Conchero-Aztec dancers often perform at the street altar and have become a big attraction for tourists in the area in a bringing together of the Aztec and Mexican images of death. While this may be seen only as the 'public face' of the cult – giving the tourists what they expect in the same way that public voodoo displays are far removed from the actual religious ceremonies – this aspect of dark tourism has gone a long way to reclaiming the figure of Santa Muerte for those who genuinely venerate her, while at the same time bringing the added commercial benefit of sales of books, magazines and the inevitable figure for your mantelpiece.

Some ceremonies or celebrations are associated with death on a much more personal level, and yet have still become cultural practices with which people now interact as 'outsiders' through a tourist experience. One of these, which takes place in a remote part of Indonesia, is the *Ma'nene* funeral rite. Largely unknown in Western cultures for many years, it has become more prominent in recent times both through articles in the tabloid press and as a featured destination in the 2018 Netflix travel documentary, *Dark Tourist*, hosted by journalist David Farrier. Both areas of the popular media would have been attracted to the somewhat bloody and morbid (in Western eyes) funerary ceremony of the Torajan people.

The Torajans, living in the South Sulawesi area of Indonesia, were an undisturbed indigenous people until the Dutch established trade routes in the area in the seventeenth century. Although now mostly Christianised thanks to interference by Dutch missionaries, some Torajans still follow the local animist beliefs, which are known as '*aluk*', meaning 'the way'.

Song, dance and ritual are an important part of the Torajan culture, as with most indigenous groups, although since being offered up by the Indonesian tourist industry as a major part of their cultural offering in the 1970s it is open to debate now what proportion of the *aluk* rites are undertaken for their original religious significance and what proportion for bringing in the tourist dollar. It is certainly true that the way that the Torajans see their own identity within the wider world has changed in the last half-century.

Funerary customs are the most important (and expensive) part of the Torajan way of life. A significant reason for this is the way that the dead are seen within that culture. Deceased family members are not seen as such until a funeral takes place, being referred to until that time as '*to makula*', or sick. This means that the family consider the person's soul as still being in the house while the body is there – and the body may remain in the home for many months before a funeral takes place. Arrangements and fundraising for such a high-status ritual may take a long time.

While caring for the 'sick' person, the family will still bring them meals and they will also accept guests into the house, which includes visiting tourists. These would be expected to give offerings of cigarettes, food or money to the sick person, via their living relatives.

Some families still follow the old *aluk* custom of ensuring that someone is always present with the body during the period before burial. Amanda Bennett, writing for *National Geographic* in 2016, shows that Torajan practices now are very much a fusion of these old ways with the Christian faith that found its way in with the Dutch. She highlights, for example, that there is often a Christian religious service before caring for the '*to makula*' person and *aluk* burial. She also describes one body being brought food and being treated with formalin to stave off putrefaction, while '[o]n the wall a picture of Jesus Christ leading a lamb looks down'.[9]

For the Torajans, death is a more important and significant event than life in many ways. They do not see death as a full stop, but rather as a transition through the veil to the next stage of a journey. This mirrors many other cultures, of course, such as the ancient Egyptian or Chinese beliefs, and we might also find parallels with the significance of funeral rites at the Ganges River in India. This does not preclude outpourings of grief, and these may be expressed periodically long after burial. This is especially true where, after death, bodies may be brought back out from their tombs many times to be re-dressed, cared for and spoken with.

This more unusual ceremony is known by the Torajans as '*ma'nene*', the 'second funeral'. Bodies will be laid out for some fresh air and sunshine and be given snacks and other goods. Family members will pose for photographs with their deceased relatives, snapping each other with the inevitable invasive smartphones now found in the Torajan community. Tourists may also have the chance to do the same. Rather than finding these events sombre, visitors report feeling very comforted by the whole experience. To a Western culture where death is so final and feared, it harks back to a time when our ancestors believed more, as the Torajans do, in the celebratory aspect of the journey to better things.

Celebration of death aside, dark tourism is often linked with the tragedy of death and suffering. Away from the sites of battle, or terrible cases of genocide, both of which offer up destinations that may be visited by a Thana tourist, there are also locations that are intrinsically connected to the taking of one's own life. One of these is Aokigahara Forest in Japan, which has become known colloquially as the 'suicide forest'.

Aokigahara is a large area of dense forest that is found at the north-west base of Mount Fuji. Covering between 30 and 35 square kilometres, it is known as a *Jukai*, translating as 'sea of trees'. Although very difficult to navigate due to its density, the forest does have a number of trails and tourist routes marked out, some of which lead to very popular caves formed as the lava from the volcano's previous eruptions hardened over time.

Locals living in the area say that there are three types of people who visit Aokigahara Forest. The first type are the normal tourists, the school parties or hikers who come to see the caves or explore the trails. The second type are the dark tourists; these are the people who come to experience the atmosphere of the area and sometimes, to try and find remaining evidence from the third type. That last group are those who do not intend to come back.

Japan has one of the world's highest rates of suicide, due in part to cultural lifestyle and the work ethic and sense of duty that Japanese citizens often have. The country also has a tradition where ritual suicide was seen as being an honourable way to end one's life. In feudal times, Japanese Samurai soldiers would perform a self-disembowelling known as *seppuku* rather than fall into enemy hands. *Seppuku* was also carried out by many officers at the end of the Second World War as being more dignified than admitting defeat. Also coming from this time are the Kamikaze suicide pilots who would voluntarily crash their planes into enemy targets.

Aokigahara Forest is a hotspot for suicide. Since the 1950s, recorded suicides have been increasing on average at a rate between 10 and 30 per cent, year on year, as far as can be ascertained (actual figures are no longer published in an effort to deter people from using the forest for this purpose). Many people ascribe the popularity of the forest for suicide to a crime book called *Nami no Tou*, or 'Tower of Waves'. Written by author Seicho Matsumoto and published in 1960, the novel concludes with a joint suicide in Aokigahara Forest. However, citing this book as the reason is one of several myths, both urban and traditional, associated with this area.

While it is true that *Nami no Tou* references the forest, it is more probable that spikes in the number of suicides are linked to the poor economic conditions in Japan. This seems to be evidenced by the fact that suicides peak in March, which is the end of the Japanese financial year. There is, in fact, a history going back to at least the nineteenth century of Aokigahara Forest being used as a location for people to bring often elderly members of their family to die. There is a practice in Japan, known as *ubasute*, of being left to die in a remote location. In times of famine, for instance, people would leave members of their family in the forest to die in order to be able to provide more food for those still at home.[10]

Writing for *Psychology Today*, Dr Frank T. McAndrew notes that suicide hotspots are not naturally creepy places in and of themselves.[11] With an estimated 2,000 deaths, the Golden Gate Bridge, spanning the strait between San Francisco Bay and the Pacific Ocean, is thought to be the world's number one location for suicides and yet very few people would class this as a dark, unnerving place. There must be other external factors at play to ascribe a spooky feeling to a suicide hotspot, which is exactly what we find at Aokigahara Forest.

The hardened lava base on which the forest sits is very porous, which means that it acts to deaden or absorb a lot of sound. This leads to the forest sounding unnaturally quiet, with only a minimal amount of birdsong. Because the soil in the area has such a high concentration of magnetic iron due to volcanic activity, compasses will behave erratically when placed on the ground. Although when carried at a normal height they point to true north quite accurately, the strange compass behaviour at low level has naturally been suggested as the norm and has been connected to other mythical stories of the area of travellers being lured from the paths by unseen forces.

There is a general belief among Japanese of a more spiritual nature that the lands of Aokigahara Forest are haunted by the souls of those who died there in the form of ghosts known as *yurai*. These spirits are often associated with traumatic deaths such as those suffered by the people who died by starvation, or by hanging:

Aokigahara yurai. *(Illustration by Kathryn Avent)*

In the Japanese popular belief, if a person dies in a deep sense of hatred, anger, sadness, or desire for revenge, their soul can't leave this world and continues to wander, appearing to people affected by the spell or those who cross his path. These souls are called yurai and they … just want to have their curse removed or conflicts resolved.[12]

The *yurai* are said to be responsible for beckoning travellers into the dense forest, causing them to leave the trails and become lost among the trees, never to come out again.

These ideas are not unlike those in fairy folklore of being pixy-led or being taken away by the fae. The idea that compasses cannot be used for navigation has also found its way into this belief, being ascribed to the *yurai* as well.

Belief in the *yurai* is still quite widespread among many Japanese. Corpses of suicide victims transformed into *yurai* are said to scream all night and move around on their own if they are left unattended and so it is considered bad luck to do so. There is a room at the edge of Aokigahara Forest where forest guards place recovered bodies before they are handed over to the police, and it is said that the guards play 'Rock, Paper, Scissors' in order to determine who will spend the night with the body. The police also have a special room that they use for suicide corpses.

Locations such as those used for suicides, those linked to tragedies that were not on a mass scale, or those associated with execution such as gallows sites are often linked with hauntings. These are often sought out by visitors through the commodification of ghost stories by tours or owners of allegedly haunted properties, or by people engaging with stories through the practice of legend tripping.

The concept of legend tripping is precisely what the semantics of the term suggest – those taking part in the trip visit a location that has a legend attached to it in the hope that they might experience the legend as if they were a part of it. It is part of a wider concept in folklore studies known as ostension.

When ostension takes place, a legend is not represented through a narrative device such as storytelling but is rather *presented* through direct action and engagement with it, such as those examples found in Chapter 4. By engaging in ostensive interaction with a legend, participants are exploring the heritage of a site in a form of historical re-enactment, thereby fulfilling part of the table of dark tourist motivations that we saw earlier. Furthermore, each ostensive action adds more to the legend that is being explored, furthering its continuity and adapting its narrative.

It is important to draw a distinction between ostension and acting. A ghost tour that tells the stories of a location or plays out some of the heritage through costumed actors is not ostensive in itself, but if it leads to an overnight stay in an alleged haunted venue for the purposes of ghost hunting, then it may be seen to become so.

Locations such as prisons, abandoned hospitals or asylums are popular locations for such tours, although they can lead to something of a contested history for a property. Nathaniel Buchanan runs ghost tours in the former Ararat Lunatic Asylum in Aradale, Australia. In the book *Aradale: The Making of a Haunted Asylum*, Buchanan discusses how he is constantly at odds with tour groups who use the building during the day to discuss the history of the venue, avoiding the darker past of medical mistreatment and death that make up a large part of his own tour.[13]

Neither group is necessarily right or wrong. They just engage with different aspects of the past in different ways. Buchanan points out that a ghost is a vehicle for telling a good story, and that people on a ghost tour have particular expectations, which they pick up through their exposure to popular culture. By engaging with the folklore in a location such as Aradale, you can use it to teach the history, just in a different way. Staff working at Aradale when it was still operational had suggested that the building was haunted, and these stories can be used to engage with the heritage:

> Sightings of the figure of an 1880s dressed 'Nurse Carey' wandering through the Female Ward had been reported by nurses on nightshift up until the asylum's closure[,] among numerous other stories. The description of this figure's clothes imparts historic detail, and does so in a far more engaging way than just a description of historic uniforms. Stories like these were reworded for dramatic impact and included in the script, yet also drew upon established representations in folklore.[14]

A location with good stories and a disturbing past is ideal for hosting a ghost tour. Dorina-Maria Buda, a Professor of Marketing and Tourism Studies at Nottingham Business School who specialises in affective and dark tourism, noted in a TEDx talk in 2017 that emotions and affects (those factors that generate a particular feeling or mood) are a driving force behind tourism generally, and dark tourism crosses the emotional binaries of fun and fear. How those emotions are manipulated depends very much on the location. While a ghost tour might be deemed acceptable in an old hospital or cemetery, it would not be suitable for exploring the history of a concentration camp.

Partaking in forms of legend tripping provides a way of being able to manage or regulate a dark tourism experience. As a form of play, interacting with a story in an environment such as a cemetery makes those taking part more sensitive to the underlying events behind a legend while they still receive an enjoyable or fulfilling experience.

Of course, there still needs to be some mediation or filter involved to ensure that things do not get taken too far. In 2004, after visiting the Black Mausoleum in Greyfriars Kirkyard to test the legend of the Mackenzie poltergeist, two teenagers were arrested for decapitating a corpse and using the head as a toy. The events were reported widely in the national press at the time. But cases such as this are an exception, and legend tripping is usually more carefully mediated by the participants so that it is not taken to extremes.

The story of the MacKenzie poltergeist is a typical example of a perfect legend trip as it encompasses many of the elements that we have already explored. Greyfriars Kirk, in Edinburgh, Scotland, is a site associated with a particularly bloody battle. The mausoleum houses the body of Sir George Mackenzie, who has earned the nickname 'Bloody Mackenzie' because of the part he played in the persecution of Covenantors during the reign of King Charles II. He is said to have overseen the torturing and ultimate death of some 18,000 Scots. Ironically, his body ended up being interred in the same kirkyard as many of his victims. All of these tropes combined have led to the formation of a standard type of legend.

A key moment in the embedding of the legend seems to have occurred in 1998 when a homeless man broke into the Mackenzie mausoleum looking for shelter. The story tells that during the night, in response to some vandalism that he was responsible for, the ground opened, and he fell into a pit full of human remains. He is said to have fled the kirkyard and nobody saw him again. (This obviously doesn't explain how the story subsequently propagated, but these are the points that we overlook in the development of a legend!) Since this, there have been hundreds of reports of unusual activity at the Black Mausoleum and so naturally it has become an attractive site for legend trippers who ascribe these goings-on to the unquiet spirit of Bloody Mackenzie.

These events are adding to a previous belief that the mausoleum saw supernatural behaviour within its walls. Legend tripping activities need a known experience to hope for evidence of, or a theory to test. Much like the children's dare of circling the tomb of Richard Cabell and putting your finger in its keyhole, which was described in Chapter 2, there is a summoning ritual for the Mackenzie poltergeist too. Rachael Ironside notes that 'local children dared each other to knock on the tomb's door and chant, "Bluidy Mackingie, come oot if ye daur, lift the sneck and draw the bar!"'[15]

This idea of ostensive play is more common than direct ostension when we look at the way people interact with these forms of legends. The percentage of participants who actively 'believe' in the legend itself is usually quite low. The fun comes from the element of the dare and the tension associated with the thought that something frightening might happen. It is again reflective of the interplay between fun and fear noted by Dorina-Maria Buda and suggestive of the reasons that legend tripping is most popular as a pastime for the 18–35 age bracket. It is also why we find that trips to haunted sites and ritualised play such as summoning Bloody Mary or the Candyman are the most common types of performance associated with legend stories.

As an example of this ostensive play in action, and a demonstration of how legend tripping expands the storied event that is being recreated by adding what happens on the trip to the core narrative of the legend itself, we will consider another gravesite – this time in the USA at the Black Angel monument in Oakland Cemetery, Iowa City.

The grave in question is that of the Feldevert family, and of particular relevance is Teresa Feldevert, who passed away in Iowa City in 1924. Local history records the details of Teresa's life and how the monument came into being:

Teresa Feldevert went to Iowa City from what is now Czechoslovakia in the late 19th century, as did many others. By her first marriage, she had a son, Edward Dolezal, who died in Iowa City in 1891,

Black Angel, Iowa City. (Photo credit: Billwhittaker at English Wikipedia)

his grave marked by the tree stump. Teresa had the bronze angel sculpted in Chicago, and it was erected in the cemetery in 1912. The ashes of her second husband, Nicholas Feldevert, were placed in a repository at its base. Teresa died in 1924, and her ashes were placed beside her husband's. The monument bears the birth and death date of Nicholas, but Teresa's birthdate only – 1836. The metal statue apparently oxidized when exposed to air, and is now almost completely black.[16]

A successful legend prospers when there is significant ambiguity attached to it, and there is certainly plenty to be found here. Teresa Feldevert's name has no date of death attached to it. Much of the inscription is in a foreign language no longer generally found in Iowa City (although it was common at the time that the Feldeverts were alive), the location of the monument is unusually prominent, and it is the only one of its type to be found in the whole cemetery. Probably most significant of all is its colour.

As was demonstrated in Chapter 4 on Urban Legends in this book, legend texts come alive in the retelling. In cases of legend tripping, the act of telling the story before visiting the site not only informs anyone attending who may not be familiar with the history of the area, but it sets the scene for all the participants and creates an atmosphere suitable for those trying to experience something supernatural or scary. This is especially true if the stories are told on the way to or at the site where the legend is based.

Stories told about the supernatural reason for the angel's colour and other aspects of the legend tend to vary according to the age or social background of the teller. This is because all narratives take on some personal elements in the telling and, hence, consciously or otherwise, become either autobiographical or include some of the cultural norms of the person explaining them.

Older adults tend to look to ideas of the angel being black in sympathy for the loss of a child or because of some other form of sorrow. Teens and twenty-somethings, on the other hand, emphasise retribution for the sins of the woman when she was alive, calling her either an adulteress or a witch. Both folklore and pop culture of young adults has a focus on themes of morality and sexuality and the stories that we see ascribed to the Black Angel are simply an older version of those that we see in stereotypical horror and slasher movies.

Where stories from older adults tend to only focus on the explanation for the monument's design, it is the ones that are told by younger people, associated with the dare aspect that we have already discussed, which generate new narratives that feed into the overall legend. This may be seen as one of the powers, or lasting effects, of the phenomenon of legend tripping.

Narratives are constantly challenged, expanded or altered as the popularity of a site increases. Through surveys of legend trippers undertaken between 1981 and 1986 by Donald F. Johnson, who was a graduate student at the University of Iowa at the time, we see many examples being shaped of darker beliefs in the power of the angel. One of these is the motif of the 'scary threat' – variations of actions that bring about consequences are touching, kissing or making fun of the angel. Retribution might come in the form of bad luck or even death in a proscribed time period. Another version warns that if you gaze into the eyes of the angel, it will put a curse on you.

There is something inherently creepy about inanimate objects shaped as something human or humanoid, and we might think, when we read these stories, of the concept of the Weeping Angels in the popular science fiction series *Doctor Who* as being surprisingly similar. Recalling how he came up with the idea, writer Steven Moffat described in an interview a visit to a hotel, which he originally believed was in Dorset but which was later shown to have actually been the Ickworth Hotel in Suffolk:

We were at a hotel in Dorset and there was a graveyard next to the hotel. The church was closed down and the graveyard gates were all chained up with a big sign saying, 'Unsafe structure'. That seemed really frightening. I went over and looked inside, and saw all these leaning gravestones and one lamenting, weeping angel. I thought that was really creepy and strange, and wondered if that was the unsafe structure.[17]

Another American gravesite that sees similar activity is that of Mercy Brown, in the Chestnut Hills Baptist Church Cemetery in Exeter, Rhode Island. Mercy has become the most well known of several deceased in southern Rhode Island who have had claims of being vampires attached to them.

The legend of Mercy Brown tells that she, her mother and her sister all died in a short space of time, and her brother Edwin fell ill with what was described as consumption. Townspeople believed that something unusual had happened and that Edwin's condition was due to a vampire. They persuaded his father to exhume all the bodies, which subsequently happened. It was found that although her mother and sister had been reduced to bones, Mercy was still only partly decomposed. Although the doctor responsible stated that the levels of decomposition were normal for the period that Mercy had been buried, and that blood found in her heart and liver was not unnatural, local residents thought otherwise. Mercy's heart and liver were burned, and the ashes were given to Edwin to consume, as folk beliefs suggested that this might effect a cure. It did not, and he died a few months later.

Mercy's grave is frequently visited by people today. Some leave offerings or light candles but others come to test the legend that Mercy's ghost can be summoned by means of a similar sort of ritual to those for Squire Cabell or Bloody Mackenzie. In this case, one should peer at her grave through a hole in another tombstone found nearby, while repeating three times the words 'Mercy Brown, are you a vampire?'. This is very reminiscent of the mirror rituals of Bloody Mary or Candyman. As with the Black Angel at Iowa City, causing offence may also have the desired effect and so people have been known to urinate on gravestones, have sex or cause vandalism in an attempt to raise the spirit of Mercy Brown. All acts such as this risk, as you would expect, some kind of supernatural ill fortune.

Both dark tourism and legend tripping are not about what people understand a legend to be, but rather what they do with it and how they interact with a site. Because of the dark nature of the subject matter and locations involved, this can be very open to misinterpretation. This is the reason that many people see such things as visits to cemeteries or abandoned churches with legends attached to them as some form of cult activity, especially where, such as in the case of Mercy Brown's alleged vampirism, subcultures who are frequently stereotyped such as Goths are naturally drawn to participation. The results are the same as those mentioned with reference to the Satanic Panic in the examination of urban legends.

Legend tripping is usually undertaken for entertainment or fun. Being frightened is a big element of many legend trips, but it is done in a safe and mediated way. Sometimes people use the legend trip to confront their own real-life fears. It should be noted, though, that in very rare and tragic cases, events are not misinterpreted and do exceed boundaries in the same way as was seen with the Slenderman stabbings. In these circumstances, ostension is taken far away from the areas of play or entertainment and the legend or folklore is used as a way of copycatting for criminal purposes.

Sometimes, this is a conscious act. In 1974, Houston resident Ronald O'Bryan used the urban myth of Halloween candy having razor blades or other dangerous substances in it as a cover story for his own poisoning of his son, leading to his being given the nickname 'Candy Man'.

Sometimes, the act is unconscious. In 1986, again in Houston, Juana Leija took a bus ride with her seven children into town. After leaving the bus, she walked them onto the bridge over Buffalo Bayou where she picked them up one at a time and threw them off the bridge. By the time locals managed to stop her, six of the children were in the water and two had drowned.

Leija was subconsciously acting out the legend of La Llorona – a woman who, angry with her husband, kills their children by throwing them into a river. It is a very well-known legend in the Houston area, particularly among the Hispanics from whose culture it emerges, and Leija admitted later that she had no idea what was going to happen when she took the children onto the bus with her.

Such events as these are rare and they are not happenings that are later marked by legend tripping. This is reserved for the sites with much older stories embedded more in folklore than recorded history, but with the requisite elements of death or tragedy feeding into the legend.

Death as a function of tourism often takes place for religious purposes. Sometimes this might be to experience a particular event, such as the Santa Muerte festivities or the Torajan *Ma'nene* ceremony, or sometimes it might be viewed as the tourist undertaking some sort of pilgrimage, not unlike the more devout Catholic example of Lourdes. When seen as a pilgrimage, the culmination of the trip needs to be meaningful to the participants on a far more personal level than the interplay with the alleged danger of something like the Black Angel or Mercy Brown's grave. And yet it still involves the same testing of the supernatural credentials of a story in the hope for an expected outcome. A classic example of this form of trip used to be found on Shane Road, at the intersection with Villamain, in the very southern part of San Antonio, Texas. This was the site of the Legend of the Ghost Tracks.

The story attached to this site is of interest not just because we find regular legend tripping here as a form of pilgrimage, but also because although the basis of the happenings here is most definitely an urban legend, it has been very strongly adopted in the Houston and San Antonio areas by the Hispanic community as a part of their heritage. Although the original page is no longer active, the website ghosts.org used to offer this useful summary of the legend type in play at the San Antonio crossing:

> Once, there was a tragic accident on a set of train tracks: A busload of children was crossing the tracks, and could not get out of the way in time to avoid the approaching train. The train smashed into the bus, killing most of the children and the driver survived. Now, if your car stalls on the tracks, it will be pushed over the tracks to safety before the train hits you. The ghosts of the children have saved you, and sometimes you can see their small handprints in the dust on your car. The most well-known example of this urban legend are the haunted train tracks in San Antonio, Texas.

There are, as you would expect, a few variations on the story – for example, sometimes the driver survives and sometimes not.

The story, that seems to have emerged in the 1970s, is one of several similar tales which are used retroactively as a proffered explanation for the seemingly impossible phenomenon of an idle car rolling uphill. The same anomaly is ascribed to the ghosts of dead teenagers whose car was supposed to have overturned on a freeway intersection in another variant. In all of the cases, the location is what is generally termed a 'gravity hill'. That is, the landscape is such that although the ground runs downhill (in San Antonio the gradient was some 2 degrees), it appears as if the ground actually rises and hence the car appears to roll uphill. With the legend attached, such an event could only be 'supernatural'.

With reference to San Antonio, there was an actual accident whose story has been used to add credence to the phenomenon, but it took place many miles away in Utah, in 1938. The details appear in an archived article on the website of *The Salt Lake Tribune* newspaper:

> On Dec. 1, 1938, a school bus was heading to Jordan High School through a dense winter storm as a loaded Denver and Rio Grande

freight train rolled north toward Salt Lake City, according to information posted on the city's website.

Near the railroad crossing at 10200 South and 400 West, the driver stopped the bus. He opened the door to look beyond the thick fog, but did not see the 80-plus car 'Flying Ute' train approaching at over 50 miles per hour.

At 8:43 a.m., the bus pulled slowly forward across the tracks. Upon seeing the bus, the train crew immediately applied the brakes, but the collision was inevitable.

The collision claimed the lives of 23 children and the bus driver. The 15 survivors faced a lifetime of serious physical injuries and emotional scars.[18]

This tragic event was covered extensively in the newspapers in the San Antonio region at the time, for a period of ten days or more, which has probably led to its embedding in that area with reference to the gravity hill.

Other local history is also used to feed into this legend. Several of the streets in the surrounding area are named after people. According to the story, these are the names of some of the children who died in the original bus accident. In actuality, the streets are all named after the grandchildren of the developer of the area.

The effect of rolling uphill on its own would be interesting enough to garner some visitors to the site, but what turned the San Antonio Crossing into a popular site for legend tripping is summed up in half a sentence about the ghosts from the legend description above: '... sometimes you can see their small handprints in the dust on your car'.

Legend tripping involves the interaction with a story in the hope of experiencing the alleged events in that legend. With the ghost tracks, the experience was guaranteed – your vehicle would certainly roll uphill. But the addition of the claim of small handprints being visible adds a chance for veracity of the story to be possible.

This potential for proof of interacting with the spirits of helpful children through the legend is what turns this particular example into something akin to a religious experience for many visitors. In some cases, people have been encouraged to sprinkle baby powder on the rear of their car to try to see the handprints. We have all seen handprints on the boot of our car in the past from the way that we grip the boot with our fingers when closing it. Often, it is only the tips of the fingers on the outside of the car and hence adult handprints can sometimes appear to be quite small. If a car was not dusty but did have greasy finger marks, which were not readily visible, sprinkling baby powder on the car could bring them out and lead to a miraculous-looking confirmation of the spirit children at work if done after the event.

The way that some visitors choose to attend the San Antonio crossing is most certainly a pilgrimage. For example, in 2001 an entire vanload of Catholic schoolgirls, in uniform, arrived at the tracks having driven 275 miles from Brownsville, Texas. After crossing the tracks in the van and experiencing the phenomenon, they drove off to make the return journey of another 275 miles.

The unique interplay of a ghost story that had a guaranteed physical anomaly connected with it has led to many individuals also engaging with it on a more spiritual level and hence making repeated trips to their personal site of pilgrimage, as they saw it. Carl Lindahl, Professor of English at the University of Houston, carried out extensive fieldwork talking to those who visited the San Antonio ghost tracks.[19]

One of his witnesses describes how, on the occasion of one visit, she had her infant daughter in the van with her alongside various other family members. It was decided that some form of 'protection' should be given to the child because they were dealing with supernatural forces and so a Sacred Heart necklace was used. Given at a First Communion, the necklace had a picture of Jesus on the reverse, opposite the Sacred Heart. The family duly parked their van in the appropriate place and witnessed the rolling over the tracks. There were no detrimental effects to the child, and so this could be seen as an affirmation of the power of the family faith.

The interplay with the story undertaken by some legend trippers who visit a site like this multiple times can be quite complex and work on many levels. In its simplest form, we see ostensive play happening, but then we also see the religious quality of that ostension on another level. Some visitors find the phenomenon calming, and almost miraculous, and identify with the concept of the spirit children doing good from the world beyond. Here, the ostension is (as Carl Lindahl suggests) almost an act of healing.

In bringing together the supernatural, ritual, a good ghost story, tragic history and the geographic anomalies leading to an event that could be witnessed, the San Antonio ghost tracks are a good example of a legend-tripping experience that really has it all. Or rather, had it all. In 2018, due to an increase in rail traffic in the area, it became necessary for railroad company Union Pacific to install a second set of tracks to create a siding to shunt trains into. As part of this development, the incline of the ground needed to be altered, meaning that the gravity hill effect no longer happened. In addition, as part of a general increase in crossing safety, lights and barriers were installed at the San Antonio site.

Legends, once they become established, are very much embedded in the culture and history of an area and so, although this act means that the physical phenomena at the crossing could no longer be experienced, it did not mean a discontinuation of the story, or of a desire to visit the site. This now just happens in a different way, often as part of 'Haunted San Antonio' organised tours or sometimes merely as a pilgrimage to visit (or revisit) a site deemed by many to have been important or culturally significant.

To many people, the concept of dark tourism is an unappealing one. This is increasingly true considering the current trends of a 'cancel culture', which is leading to the removal of reminders of our cultural history, rather than acknowledgement and interpretation that they were wrong and that, although they are far from part of desirable societal norms in the twenty-first century, they still happened and should be explained or remembered. To remove them completely is to deny a narrative to the victims.

By visiting sites in Vietnam, the Choeung Ek Killing Fields in Cambodia, or Auschwitz-Birkenau in Poland, tourists are directly engaging with the memories of the past, acknowledging wrongs and partaking in a shared experience across time that continues to shape the narratives of those locations. It may not appeal to many, but that does not make it inappropriate. Rather, it provides a chance to interact with our heritage and shape the direction that it takes in the future. One survivor of the Vietnam atrocities said, in a documentary on dark tourism produced by filmmaker Manfred Becker, that they wanted tourists to come and visit and that they would feel very sad if they did not.

Any folkloric text is inherently empty until it has meaning ascribed to it through the context into which it is placed, or the way that it is read or used. The power of a legend is that it can both make and transform a place through the way that people interact with it. Through legend tripping and play, many people harness the perceived negative potential of ostension in a folk narrative and, like those who made pilgrimages to witness the miracle of ghost children pushing their car, turn it to a personal or cultural positive.

REFERENCES

1 Foley, M. and J.J. Lennon, 'JFK and Dark Tourism: A fascination With Assassination', *International Journal of Heritage Studies*, 2(4) (1996).
2 Soni, G. and S. Hussain, 'Dark Tourism: Changing Perception of Travelers for Indian Tourism', *Omniscience*, Vol. 8, No. 3 (2018).
3 Stone, P., 'A dark tourism spectrum: towards a typology of death and macabre related tourist sites, attractions and exhibitions', *Tourism* 54(2) (2006).
4 Dogancili, O.S., *Current Issues in Tourism and Hospitality Management*, (SRA Academic Publishing, 2019).
5 www.tajmahal.org.uk/legends/third-graves.html (Accessed 1.3.21)
6 Bigley, J.D., et al., 'Motivations for War-related Tourism: A Case of DMZ Visitors in Korea', *Tourism Geographies*, 12(3) (2010).
7 Venbrux, E., 'Cemetery tourism: Coming to terms with death?', *Folkloric Research* (61) (2010).
8 Kingsbury, K., 'Death is Women's Work: Santa Muerte, a Folk Saint and her Female Followers', *International Journal of Latin American Religions* (2020).
9 Bennett, A., 'When Death Doesn't Mean Goodbye', www.nationalgeographic.com (accessed 9.3.21).
10 www.tsunagujapan.com/aokigahara-the-suicide-forest-in-japan (accessed 9.3.21).
11 McAndrew, F.T., 'The Creepiness of Japan's Suicide Forest', www.psychologytoday.com (accessed 9.3.21).
12 www.tsunagujapan.com/aokigahara-the-suicide-forest-in-japan (accessed 9.3.21).
13 Waldron, D., et al., *Aradale: The Making of a Haunted Asylum* (Arcadia, 2020).
14 *Ibid.*
15 Ironside, R., 'The Allure of Dark Tourism: Legend Tripping and Ghost Seeking in Dark Places', in Dennis Waskul and Marc Eaton, *The Supernatural in History, Society and Culture* (Temple University Press, 2018).
16 Bird, S.E., 'Playing with Fear: Interpreting the Adolescent Legend Trip', *Western Folklore*, Vol. 53, No. 3 (1994).
17 otralala.blogspot.com/2018/01/st-marys-ickworth-inspiration-for.html (accessed 11.3.21).
18 *The Salt Lake Tribune*, 'Memorial to mark 1938 crash that killed 23 students', archive.sltrib.com/article.php?id=57173748&itype=CMSID (accessed 17.3.21).
19 Lindahl, C., 'Ostensive Healing: Pilgrimage to the San Antonio Ghost Tracks', *The Journal of American Folklore*, Vol. 118, No. 468 (2005).